ZOLAND POETRY

AN ANNUAL OF POEMS

ZOLAND POETRY

TRANSLATIONS & INTERVIEWS

Edited by
ROLAND PEASE

ZOLAND BOOKS
An imprint of Steerforth Press
Hanover, New Hampshire

CONTENTS

INTRODUCTION

In assembling this collection I had one main goal: Present poems from many countries and aesthetics, having as large a range of excellence as possible. In this day and age of constant conflict around the world it seems to me language is our greatest resource, maybe our only salvation. I don't expect this book to bring about world peace (though if it does all the better), but if you the reader find much to linger over, digest, enjoy, react for or against, poems to reread and share with friends, then I have done my job.

My mission for Zoland Poetry is the same as it was for Zoland Books (the literary publishing company I directed for fifteen years): Bring into print work that I believe matters, work by new as well as veteran writers, writers who take me by storm. And in the same way Emile Zola's last name flowed into my first name, I see a political side in everything around me, know it to be true. I look to his work as a guide to my own. All things are political, even words, maybe even especially words, and literature can help us see and feel and think more than before, more than ever. Listening and learning will never go out of style, so even if the world of technology surrounds us and takes away potential readers, they always come back to read poems at weddings and burials. And they probably write poems under the cover of darkness too.

As Denise Levertov once said, "One of the obligations of the writer, and perhaps especially of the poet, is to say or sing *all* that he or she can, to deal with as much of the world as becomes possible to him or her in language." When I chose writers for Zoland Books and now Zoland Poetry, from Kevin Young and Anne Porter to Ha Jin and William Corbett to Ange Mlinko to Patricia Smith to Dean Young and others, I was aware that they were holding nothing back. I expected nothing less from them, and I applaud their reach and ability to deliver what was needed.

I want to place credit where credit is due. My first thanks go to the poets who have given this collection strength. If you enjoy a particular poet's work I encourage you to support them by reading more of their work, by buying their books. Poets are important and deserve our attention. Great thanks go to Christopher Mattison, who from the very beginning of this project has opened my eyes to the world of translation. I told Cris in putting together this book one of my goals was to learn and I have done so beyond measure. If the collection works it's because Cris and I have worked well together (and had fun in the process). Thanks also go to Chloe Garcia Roberts who assisted with the editorial process and is our book-review editor for the website—www.zolandpoetry.com—(which will run quarterly reviews of poetry collections, the original languages of translated work in each annual, audio clips of select poets, and various other updates). Thanks also to all the other contributing editors who have led me to poets and poems I never knew existed. I thank them one and all.

On a personal note: I want to thank my daughter Anna whose comprehension of lively writing pleases me no end. She is the ideal reader for this collection. To my son Nat who gave me great advice: When I was considering a different literary direction he steered me clear of it by saying, "Chance of a lifetime? A chance to ruin a lifetime." And to my wife Lori who has been the guardian angel of all things Zoland.

—Roland Pease

ZOLAND POETRY

JÓNAS ÞORBJARNARSON

*from Icelandic by Astradur Eysteinsson
& Julian Meldon D'Arcy*

Original Language

I.

The sea spoke to me

a boat interjected

a bird too

and that whiteness from afar

a white mountain

the sea spoke to me

I listened, trying not to understand

listening like the shoreline listens

trying not to translate the world into language

2.

The sea continued
speaking calmly to me

and I continued
listening and keeping still

not unlike
a gentle man soothing a cat

Camping on Langanes

A long peninsula that slung
people out

in search of bird   fish   life

and further, not a soul
but overgrown ruins:

the other side of good days

my tent is now being raised …
not the most promising settlement

my tent, the midsummer light

The Lighthouse in Hjalteyri Shining

The rush of bygone herring catches …
well in the past now, a gray factory silence

a pier so decrepit
only jellyfish dock

it is not out of cruelty that I spit at them
simply the need for action; there's not much else to do

the house I'm renting stands alone on a hill
built during the first world war

when I press my ear to the floor there's distant thunder
or heartbeats

when I glance at the photos of those who've lived here
I'm looking into the eyes

of a long-bearded unreality
and his wife

and what do they see in me, is it certain
that I am what's real?

half numb from the stillness and the past
I'm unsure

the lighthouse is the only sign of life
acting as if a ship is nearby

best to do like the lighthouse: talk
so that my picture won't fade

say something …
pretend I'm not alone

In the Mountains, There You Feel Free

Here kissing lasts a country mile.
Here idiot blooms and tenderness raked.

Somewhere in the sun we have lost
our way and settled inside a gilded maw.

Virgins and tykes grip the clover for ballast.
Crones doubled-over speak to their sores.

Together we go lordless on a breeze
like bells on the loose which all of a sudden
soften the silence with ghostly peals.

I run my silver down your parts.
You run your silver down mine.

What vessels we are, what sad lace maps
worn out by direction, trading on the past.

I hustle my tears for a view from your eyes.
The peak of every color shouting each to each.
The sun has a body to go with its head.

Argument

Like you nature pimps me to the handiest god.
One that butchers light to make more of it.
Fattens it first with feeling so none goes to waste.
None, none, my dear, none none
is a song we sing ourselves to sleep,
sleep itself a leaky refrain, a hand
that skims the wheat before plot intrudes,
a lukewarm heiress, a marriage annulled
to elope with a color, sovereign as a beast.
Once my difference made me bold
but now it is my sameness. A good poem
shoots me like trash into space
and the rags I call mother fall into the sea.
Like you, I say goodbye to my mother
who gave me a cry which was long and loud
it sent love running along its length.
Like you, I need a stranger to tend me in death.
Only a stranger will do.

Enemy Love Song

You are a beautiful tense with no language to live in
and a mean pathological slit-show with no stuff to disperse
or mirror to break into flower
when I put words in your mouth like this harness itches
these tits leak indecipherable speech I unchain the animals
and place them sleeping around you for everyone
should experience their ass brushing your face
at least once in a lifetime I saw you soaking in grass
until grass no longer felt its sex and I shouted
smite me like a nation it is you
who washes death's small posable head with soft licks
one day you will lick it entirely away for it is tasty
licking an entire salt woman advancing world peace
I brush against your face and sworn enemies
explode into talcum powder blooms

Them Is Us

don't be watchin
the skies keep

your eyes
on the North

Pole the living
vegetable

you can eat
him if he don't

eat you first

The Hip Bone

Ethel Waters as Bernice in "Member of the Wedding"

in heaven she never leaves the kitchen
the apron round her waist
a grin that says every day comes from God

and her own good natured self
over the stove she fries and flips
pancakes from old southern living

corn Paul Lawrence Dunbar and dry bones
by the stove dreams of home (she calls her crib)
or in the late evening quietly

goes to Niggertown to the craps
the laughing no-good men
the bad news slick men the coroner's report

the people the sweet girls and their gin
in heaven in the kitchen
Bernice mama oh mama mine

Ginsberg

Hoover is on the phone
he's got your number

and mine
mother

Ginsberg the Jew
finds Auschwitz

in the streets
on Times Square

mother listen
to the voices

in the walls
you are not

crazy Naomi
the bombs

are falling
the Rosenbergs

are writing
love letters

mother Hoover

is on the phone
reading

the Rosenberg
letters

calling

my poems
insane

About the Expatriate Jazz Musician Steve Lacy, after Seeing Portraits of Han-shan and Shi-te

Others may hold the scroll, you
may have the broom, loony sage,
bath water just right now,
and you roll around in that
which is your homely broom.
Steve Lacy looks like some detective
retirement cardigan, Palm Springs,
balding from porkpies,
grandpa admittance, lonesome
applications and reaches: soprano sax,
Detective Steve Lacy, Paris
gendarme, golfs a bit, goofs
the hotel setting, the disappointed
raspberry sauce off the cake plates
all the long table wants to scrape at,
fork at, prolong,
so the long table files out
like 7th inning at Dodger Stadium
that misses how to live here.

At the Mashantucket Pequot Museum

It's worth a lot of purple, inner clams,
this cheerful version of innocence.
Village mannequins have very good tone,
like Clinique counter ladies.
This village indoors, in eastern Connecticut,
is Polynesia. I love that there's so much skin
involved with the transmission
of skills. I think of the great heavy breathers
of innocence. It's always May recreated,
under the corn-hung rafters.
These villagers did lots of leaping around,
but they also had some steam huts.
Nobody was fat. The small of the back
is so graceful, much sexier
for the half-flayed deer, the split trout
on the wooden hibachi by the pond.
The woman on the stand in the cornstalks
holds aloft a rock to smash rabbit or crow.
Although there are no tabby cats here,
everybody should have these woodland sounds
piped into his or her own neighborhood.
We should keep dusty rhododendrons
and the mountain laurel always in bloom.
Even the mutts are trim and healthy.
You use blunt arrows to merely stun
the squirrel on the elm tree.
Off to the side, a few young guys share
long pipes. It must have been pretty boring,
but at the same time intensely exciting.
It's like there are all these showgirls
backstage doing their things, and the hoods
hang out in the alley, subsisting in pleasure.
I feel like gambling and getting laid myself
in the privacy of the corn stand.
Then I want a bag of fried smelts.

Getting Sick & Better

My engaged friends understand
despair and all, pretty well,
no doubt. They also know
summer. When they hear
this archaic desk calendar
of a phrase, they get intrigued.
The thing has ropes and sandbags
attached to it. They can go up
and down into the brown places
above the stage. They can swing
on it awhile, enough vine
to support some weight back
and forth for a few moments.
In happiness, everybody walks
around saying, "So where do you
come from?" You feel glad
about Fellini, Mastroianni
and Masina. When it's all
odd jobs, horrible life,
anyplace is pure fenestration.
There's a blazer from last night
draped over the back of a desk chair.
There are crumbs from raisin toast
in the saucer, a soiled eyelid
at the bottom of the cup. The radio
can't come in very clearly.
The clock on the night table
says something different than
the clock on the wall. You lie out
in the gray openness, second
week in August, rainy,
West End Avenue. Your friends
are all on vacation and busses
feel emptier. Rush hour won't
hurry much, in the marbled

vault lobby of the Lucerne.
Winds come here dismantling
the dandelions up to the infield
and alongside empty bleachers.
Sabrina would rob liquor stores
like some saxophone player
when she feels the way I do
and when I feel like her
and what goes in the mail pile
with the trade newsletters
of dry cleaners and laundries.
I'll be happy when she gets
to the yard with her clippers
and spade, and the garden
looks alright again in the sun,
and I come back up the street,
the actual one we live on
and see her sit still, breathing
in the front yard and weeds.

Sonnet—to Central & Sacred Heart

As slow, as inexorable, a sort of bee made of rain eating a canal
along the curve of a pear, mourning any beautiful orchards
into a vast house of hieroglyphics: even so I am not listening
to golden notes that could be skimming just above the waters
with their mouths open, the terns diving by the pools. Hawks circle
at the last inlet on the Jersey cape then. Out in back of apartments,
an unheated indoor porch, paint buckets with their sloppy lips
and metal handles rusting are part of the doubling up life, the festival.
At swine-fests and churchgoing, everybody gets some crackling festivity.
I almost forgot about my dream of cremation, buildings in cemeteries,
not just the airbrushed sides on a van, sword fights down the winding
castle wings. Hands that have sewn patches on denim jackets, smelling
of rain, cigarette smoke, my stoned brothers, other astringents roughly
blooded with damp cotton balls, what's it like to drink fresh breast milk?

HUGO MUJICA
from Spanish by Joan Lindgren

What Has Been Given Us

there are days when at evening
life tells us
something of the pardon we're granted

which others have left unspoken.

there are nights when some vestige
lights up:

some ember in the memory, a cricket
beyond the window
or a flower
open
when the rest remain closed.

they are the nights when the quiet reveals
the life I've been given
without even the violence
                    of having deserved it

the who knows why or what,
                    pure existence, the miracle.

Only a Few Days Ago

only a few days ago my father died,
so much in so few days.

he fell weightless,
like eyelids closing at nightfall
or like a leaf, cradled,
not swept away by the wind.

today's rain is not like other rains
today it rains for the first time
                        on the marble of his tomb.

under each rain
I could be lying, I know now,
now that I have died in another.

In the Houses

Slowly it turns almost black
the nakedness
               of the blue;

stretched out on a road
a dog
howls at the silence.

Inside the houses
windows are closed,
           the kindling is lit

the day gone over in memory.

Inside life:
hunger and memory
               night and hope.

Whirlwind

The wind whistles
        along the streets;

blows
and drags a leaf
curled with thirst,

        dried of hope.

Death happens but once,
        and each time it's everyone's death.

Within

No wingbeats on high
presage
        destinies

nor does the distant train
leave a wake
(so distant
so as not to be heard)
        as it crosses the plain;

nearer, more within or
more now

there's a house, deserted
        but locked

as if afraid of nobody:
as if embracing itself
        with its own arms.

Shores

outside a dog barks

at a shadow, its own echo
or at the moon
to lessen the cruelty of distance.

it is always to escape that we close
a door,
the desert is nakedness without promise

the distance
of being near without touching
like the edges of the same wound.

inside won't fit inside,

they are not my eyes
that can look me in the eye
they are always the lips of others
                that tell me my name.

Epitaph

Tooth for a tooth, defang
The rest is gum
Plucked feather mess
Ring formation around the precious gone

We, the child of you and me

Two roots anchored each other
Each, both tree and soil

Day and night: lips played at missing
Twilight, a lasting, a last

The dyad caught in a snag
The vectors pulled
Two ends of a rope knew they were one when they tried to separate

Our future sense created a telescope
The telescope became a passage
Our passage
If it doesn't have a passage I won't call it a home

Easier to lose someone to death—the orgasm, final—than to life: the present pollutes the past, the physical blocks the view, the clatter frightens the presence

When the shutter sprang
We captured our stuffed animal
Stiff gloat of headstones

Horripilation on the plum tree
One sudden fruit, tiny impoverished seed inside

Those days of bottoms-up hourglass
Now the reverberations, the deepwalking

Doors missing from frames
Wind skeleton key
Swollen cheeked wallpaint
The taunted house

We took our shoes off and walked. The fender became a reef, garland of shells. Crabs closed their eyes like a loud wish pretending to have disappeared when we went closer. I watched as you waited a little longer —the high tide closed in quickly around your feet, covered the bare sand and picked up the backwater.

Calling

A fierce pea wanted to break the pan
The pan broke because the lid was shut and the fire constant
By then the pea

"Blindfolded for your own protection."
"What use if the fog clears when I won't need it!"
"A blind man may see once, but having seen returns to blindness. As for revelations, you need a seer."

Spinning the spider coagulated in the centre
Quickly everyone slung their washing over the lattice
Glory's fool began to vibrate very fast, longing to be stung before his time

God break my wrists and snap my knuckles so
my leaves can cheer in the wind though
my body's rooted

Oh I know God waits for me in the palace
But I am busy with his garden roses
Dazed, fiery, I take to their cool nectarine pastures
Forgetful of the closing skies

Did I ask for a red carpet that you walk into a plantation and tenderly sparing
the roses pluck all the thorns to lay upon my walkways

On a drip tarantic heart red rosary
Love soft and deli (cloud blossom) it stipulates lite rolling pads of fingers, lips
Ripe pomegranate seeds in stainless peristalsis
Milking the erect nipples of God for a glass of fully-flown gold-rose light

Spine re-curved into a bow almost humble
Voice jumping to be bowstring
My weight just before you raise me to your arm's taut radius
Shuddering like the bow of a ship ready
At the thought of what you aim me at I nearly swoon
And stay awake to a hissing twisting knife-wedge wind

One of my oars was not far enough. The other a stick to stir with.
A ghost ark drew up. A hitchhiking tree waved two bare arms above the deluge.
The last I remember was wet prints of your feet walking on water toward me
and a sign from your hand must have pushed.
The current—
The opening softening wood of my body—

As though I have been transplanted in deeper soil. Now the faces do not float
past in my dreams. They touch me and the voices stay, shivering on my skin.
Questions I held fall from my lifted hands
I whose legs were in a knot over the title of the dance

Allegro Tristamente

How do you know time isn't
the tacet, and
space the realistic mode of determining what will and won't
fulfill the requirements?

What would you say to
less fuss about the moon and
consequent toppling … you with the aggrieved landscape
sliced into oak leaves and hailstorms of pinks.

For Beverly Kenney

Anything fiery
or coming right out and carrying,
the spread of base blue,
the flake, insert a toothpick.

So who are you to flatten like a worldling
until like Beowulf one is invited to lunch.
Man takes off jacket in effort to increase wingspan. Success!
And the wind muscles the stars around.

Holy Sonnet

1.

Do something like the eyebrow colonials
coming into their own.

2.

The chrome of the new, carefully
wiped down to exclude hangers-on (it looks like but
it isn't the case that the worst is past, from
a healthy enough interest in being
to an almost pathological distrust of non-being)
who do the smearing.

3.

At such times the dander moves over. A hole in a building
could be a verb as well as an office romance.
Move the speck. It doesn't have to be
a Baltimore oriole, bursting and blooming.

It Was You Charlie

Available,
duos, from you you and you

bopping along the swag.
Which gives way
this time but ... more in topgallants.

   *

The moonlight foils a quietist
a century alit along
with a billboard.
Procedurals roar. The point in long shots coming clean

nestled in the topgallants.

SILKE SCHEUERMANN
from German by Chris Michalski

the fountain of wonder

as soon as the last curtain
in front of which we'd
meticulously carry out our rituals
had fallen over the twilight

as soon as the unconscious stage
was taken down
sick of the repetitions
of itself

and the scene had finally
collapsed

as soon as someone claims there's
still a chance

the private theater just has to
extend itself
push out into society
where water should be easy to find

and has a certain power ...

fish would swim around under the stone lions
and the rage we once thought
was holy would be oh so easily extinguished

as soon as someone asks—are you ready?
join your voice
to the waves and jump.

the nights in paris were only long because of the usual overly high expectations

i. atlantis

just don't move a muscle. otherwise the water will flow
further off towards the shore where in the sea spoken
all the coastal residents' prayers
have gathered, single syllables ground to
pixels giving birth to a black deeply
moved by tears. the sea
is slowly growing helpless from
all the depraved desires and then
like anachronistic children the coastal residents have
started trying to catch the gods again.
they might get snagged on
the flimsy aloe-scarf-like fishing rods—
clam hearts, little tiny squids
that always look in with those stupid round
yellow eyes. eyes like marbles.
eyes like when a knife
cuts into flesh as
the flesh jerks back. consents
like a professional applauder
at his own execution.

those are the fishermen i was
telling you about as we lied heart to heart like dissected
vows, stared at each other hungry and wet. maybe we could
have put down a little sushi.
i said the island's waiting
quiet
and
empty.
night hangs down a flag suspended from other
planets crashes down right in front of us
alone and forsaken in a massive pool

of water towards the shore
where everything that's ever been rejected
gathers. shoes and swords and here and there
far too daring messages in bottles that sank.

ii. on the pier

do you see the fishermen standing
over there, dazed, patient as
pilgrims as they tie their
offenses up in
little bundles
before the ships pull in
to collect everything.

they've turned so slowly mute that they can
hardly still be counted
and you see their shoulders roll
on the fragile gangplanks.

the water is kind and keeps quiet
though inside it curses at the wait.
but we won't cast off our backpacks
with guilt. do you remember
how all those black butterflies got
on our lifelines
surfing around?
how we then crushed them?

iii. but we didn't abandon our posts either

just don't move a muscle. otherwise there'll be holes in the darkness
where the light pokes restlessly around
like fingers
in a wound.
night hangs down a flag
suspended from other

planets. down here, down here it's easy to love because you
don't see the stranger's face distorted let alone
its asymmetry.

just don't move a muscle. otherwise the darkness here in the
hotel will rip open. here where it's enough to make
love every three or four weeks without
having to nurture or feed it.
where one body under
another is a landscape—
small, easy to grasp.

it's so easy all you have to do is
touch yourself for a second and the
effect is much louder than a
normal prayer.

the obsession with having a past warmed the rocks

we ask the body of the lioness lying there
what does the beloved sphinx prodigious stone
say about work. must be lonely
keeping watch or
when everything's shattered
to tiny little puzzle pieces
and only our fantasy goes on putting it back together.

dear sphinx the sunken city is
gone to seed with boredom and
the last of the pictures
you saved are
for you just faces pock-marked by plagues,
are just sand in the paws,
recognizable only in traces
still nineveh or not.

ruins too are just overgrown miracles or
are so good they can stretch themselves out sideways
into our dauntless
romantic imaginations.
unbelievable how we give ourselves addresses
there that rather officiously resemble those of the dead.

arms up and down. legs up and down
we go walking. we
talk. we make movies.
we drink yellow soda pop
without saying a word and then these
skins of stone filled out with a strangely
fluid present.

PHIL CORDELLI

Calcium Night Light

(After Ives)

Pond our first birth

of the cumulative
form a slow out-of-doors march

Piano trust over sparrow
enlarged plain chant

the idea of concord,
verdant west redding

magical frost waves

to walls for active communists

Our fists pound flat

poverty men refresh in dance
waste free and full tax
trick us

the guns of august
crisp us

attics,
attack us,

awful free

ways a badly infected
ear clear waters lie low

like sick
crystal twichell

harmony tide forever
hill each hideaway

I have written,

but never heard it

polyglot incantation

siya ay nakatayo sa balikat ng bundok
she stands upon the mountain's shoulders
langit ay kulay ng ginto at dugo
sky's the color of gold and blood
sumisigaw siya ¡mira! ¡el sol!
see how the sun weeps
tingnan mo! umiiyak ang araw!
how this mountainslope burns
nag-aapoy siya rin
sky's the color of black pearls
iyan lagi ang sa aking panaginip
this have i prophesized
ang mukha ng araw ay umiiyak

and what are these glyphs
wikang matemátiká
some human machinery
símbólo, enkantada, o gayuma
maker of souls and tongues
anong pisi o balat ng ahas
what twine or serpent skin binds
silangan at kanluran
pearl of the orient
esta punto del embarco
fractured archipelago
ang mga anak mo ay nakakalat
your children have scattered
cielo el color de perlas negras
do not forget that they have names
may sariling pangalan ang aming diwata

pananaghoy

ay, ay!

bodies disassembled in church courtyards were mango blossom
boughs knotted, hewn from roots with dull blades, catching the moon
in curlicues of fragrance. those nights, the moon was blood, and
sometimes she'd close her eyes. sometimes so much poetry, prayers on
the parched lips of dying men, forced her to hide. even the barest trees
were always good for hiding, and solitary night herons' wings' swift
slicing through cloud. how they'd lacerate sky, and how the sky bled,
bending in arcs and wisps after the bombs fell. the stillness terrified us
all. and those very veiled women who prayed with rose-scented rosaries
opened their legs for so little rice and fish. yes, this, i saw. and with my
own eyes, this i see still.

ay, ay!

*

the river spirits no longer bathe here. though in moonlight, my eyes
trick me sometimes, and i think it is the weeping tree spirit i see. i
think it is her, seducing the hunter. but instead, young bloated bodies
sleeping in the riverbed greet me as they surface.

tell me, why would the diwata visit this dead, filthy place, to make a
home among its broken things, to drink its filthy water, to breathe its
acrid air?

no, there is no more reason for her to return to this place. we may as
well fill it with mud and forget, for there is nothing but wordless burial
here. and no one who will say grace.

*

how i no longer believe in pious women. i am certain something
tawdry, a craving for stiletto heeled patent leather, perfume of tiger
lilies and tobacco, of venom, to swig from the whiskey bottle, leaving
rings of whore red lipstick, evidence of the carnal slithers beneath their
pallor. i am certain their forked tongues press hard against their palates
so that strings of profanity remain caged, a virgin's thighs shut tight. i
am certain that rough neighborhoods' wafting aromas, sticky nightclubs
of glittery g-stringed putas, of gold-toothed criminals with teardrop
tattoos make their hearts flutter, curl their hands into manicured talons,
move their tongues to lick shiny bicuspids. all the while, their lips
pursed in feigned disdain. i do not believe in pious women, but the red
imprints of corset, pale lace, and garter upon breathing, hot flesh.

oh, but how i have strayed. from my story, how i have strayed.

SARAH FOX   ANGE MLINKO

Each with recent books out through Coffee House Press and still very early in their respective poetic lives, Sarah Fox and Ange Mlinko have garnered considerable and deserved praise: "A fine-grained light like that of a 19th-century Danish landscape painting … Mlinko leads us through a mysterious space where cultural references and private recollections mingle and metamorphose into startling, dreamlike atmospheres…" said John Ashbery. And Fanny Howe on Sarah Fox: "This is how the theory of relativity begins to manifest itself in the poetry of our time…. In this new poetry we can begin to trace the way our thinking behaves."

In the following conversation for Zoland Poetry, Fox and Mlinko discuss the possibility and pitfalls of a "populist avant-garde," motherhood entwined with the dead space between manuscripts and the anxiety of making it new.

Ange Mlinko: Having one of my own, I love the babies in your poems. How did you become a doula? How long have you been doing this?

Sarah Fox: I've been a doula for four years. I'm the oldest of six children, have always been surrounded by babies, and also feel completely at ease with babies and children and pregnancy. I had my daughter almost 16 years ago and despite less than optimal circumstances (she was four weeks early, her father was far from supportive or kind, I was fairly young) I had a remarkable birth experience—only 6 hours of labor, no meds, very easeful, very empowering. A few years ago many of my friends started getting pregnant, and I found myself very drawn to them, wanting in some way to facilitate a powerful birth experience for them, and to support them after their babies were born. My sister—a nurse—suggested I might look into being a doula. I was on a Bush Artist's Fellowship, so I had spare time and money to pursue such a thing, and it inspired me. As a doula, I hope to encourage my clients' intuition and trust in themselves and their abilities, and help calm any fears, or decode any mysteries, imposed by the medical model. I care deeply about the welfare of children, and being a doula allows me to advocate for children even before they are born.

AM: Do you feel your book could be read fruitfully by your clients? Do you feel that you write *for them* actually? I'm asking because I feel that being a poet is actually an obstacle to connecting with other people, and yet I remember Bernadette Mayer mentioning in an interview that when she lived in small-town New England, her neighbors, her doctor, her butcher, etc. read her books (*Midwinter Day* and/or *The Golden Book of Words*) with great interest.

SF: Many of the births I've done have been with people who are already friends of mine, who already know me primarily as a poet (several of my clients are writers themselves). The other clients have a vague notion that I also write and teach poetry, and maybe they'll read my book. But I have never thought that the poems in *Because Why* were meant specifically for an audience of pregnant women. I do sometimes give my doula clients poems, or even books of poetry—for example, Hoa Nguyen's chapbook *Red Juice* is one I'd definitely share, Catherine Wagner's *Macular Hole*, even some of Bernadette Mayer's *The Desire of Mothers to Please Others in Letters* seems highly relevant to pregnancy, etc.—depending on what they seem to need or connect to.

I guess actually I don't believe that poetry/"being a poet" is an obstacle to connecting with other people—in fact I believe the opposite. I'm not surprised that Bernadette Mayer's neighbors enjoyed her books, especially if, living in Small Town New England, she actually knew her neighbors! I think people are curious about each other, and are, in general, hungry for insight, for what other people *think*, for what poetry might instruct or inspire.

Writing poetry is, at least for me and for most people I know, solitary. I do feel though, when I am writing it, that I am attempting to communicate, that I am reaching out to others to share in my adventure of "making," that poems depend on readers, and that this is a vital connection. And if nothing else, I very much do feel connected to the poetry community here in the Twin Cities. Most of my friends are poets, my husband (John Colburn) is a poet—most meaningful connections I make with people are because of poetry.

Let me ask you a question along these same lines because I think this is an interesting and important topic: You wrote in your Artist's Statement (for *Starred Wire)* that your audience is "anyone who knows the field of poetry well, especially the New York School," and I wonder if you doubt that non-poets would read or appreciate your work. Do you maintain any hope of reaching a broader audience? Do you think the project of poetry is always this limited? Do you feel that blogging, for example, allows you to connect (if at all) to people with less obstacle than poetry?

AM: I try not to make any assumptions about who will enjoy my work—poets, nonpoets. But I also know that few people come to my work—any work—without assumptions, some of which work against me. As the art critic TJ Clark says, "Modernism is our antiquity," and I am a romancer of American Modernism.

Do I think the project is limited? I do. When I was a child listening to country music in the back of my mother's Buick, I would get incensed at the songs that didn't give you the whole story, that ended in ambiguity. But that was the real thing, that was my education. What you leave out (and here I think, as I so often do, of Creeley's "Histoire de Florida," where the refrain goes "You left them out") is what makes it poetry.

SF: Poets I think are often unwilling to admit that the project is limited, but clearly it is and has been for a very long time! My husband likes to dream about a "populist avant-garde," and I do too, but in the end I'm not sure how "in-demand" such a poetics could become. Maybe hip-hop and spoken word are taking on this project now?… Then again maybe demand isn't so important, especially these days when it seems insurmountable just to draw attention to the truth of what's really being said around us all the time!

We are in agreement about ambiguity—obviously, as we refer to it here, not equivalent with something like *deception*. In fact it is what I want first to teach my students to embrace, to leave open that space for imagination and interpretation—a kind of freedom—that makes it art. Students are often terrified of exploring what they don't know, or what seems wild, weird, intuitive, spontaneous, experimental, in their own imaginations, and their teachers are equally if not more terrified of ambiguity. I find it immeasurably enjoyable to watch students awaken to this in their writing. I try to impress upon students how liberating, and pleasurable, it is to read poetry from a place of accepting ambiguity as well. David Shapiro gave a lecture at the Walker Art Center a few years ago on Jasper Johns, and in it he quoted Ashbery saying something like, "People want to get the meaning out of a poem, they want to open it like a can and pour it out." I love this! In my mind, this practice leads to real truth in ways that rhetoric or sentiment simply cannot.

I had never thought of my life as being "highly integrated," or recognized that integrating the various strands of my life was actually a goal, but ultimately I guess it is, however subconsciously. My life often feels very fragmented to me in fact—I teach in lots of different settings to very different kinds of students (in the public schools, in private schools, at adult workshops, at Head Start centers, for pregnant and parent teens, composition classes to English language learners)—and also do literacy work and curriculum development for Head Start, in addition to being a doula.

How do you accommodate your poetry? Does having your son make a difference in the style of your writing, or when you write, or how often, or what's at stake? Many women my age have only just now had their babies, and I have friends who have virtually stopped writing altogether in the wake of having children. Perhaps they will come back to it, perhaps not. It never felt like a choice to me, and I suspect you feel the same. Even though I was a single mother for the first ten years of my daughter's life, I never stopped to think that it might behoove us both if I gave up poetry. I'd be interested in your experience if you have anything to share. Do you read poetry to your son? Does your son know that you're a poet?

AM: Your book has such a warm human quality (without being overly specific about the details of your life)—at times when I saw the influence of Notley or Howe I felt how much gentler your dissonances were—you seem to have a wellspring of faith in the maternality of the universe. I don't know if this rings true to you, or if you even consciously control the persona in your work. That's a tricky question I suppose—nobody wants to admit to too much manipulation, but since poets don't make up characters and stories, we draw on ourselves in myriad ways, confusing the issue of inside and outside, influence and self, fiction and reality.

Anyway, the main reason I don't teach is money. I moved to New York after graduate school, and adjunct teaching is too brutal here. I ended up doing technical writing. While I detest office environments, there are aspects of technical writing I find very soothing: I take ready-made content and organize it and typeset it. I get to exercise logic and rigor. And best of all, I get to put it aside and forget about it and come fresh to poetry afterwards.

Then I wake up on my "days off" and they're not my days off: they're the days I have to craft a space for writing, not only poetry but correspondence (I put a Teletubbies DVD in for my son before I sat down to write this; as we speak, he has already gotten bored with it and is pushing his truck around the house; I keep my ears open).

On balance, I think it's easier to be a poet while raising a baby than while working an office job forty hours a week. Any job where you get to hang around the house, in spite of possible distractions, is easier on the soul.

After a while, I become impatient with the whole topic of motherhood and writing. Are those the two poles of my identity now? If so, do they really—should they really—meet? I'm still new at this motherhood business, and it's so intense, sometimes I want to put it in a box and put it away for a few hours. Poetry lets me do that. Poetry isn't interested in my motherhood necessarily. And I find that a huge relief.

There's a certain didacticism in always expecting poetry to un-cover something about the self. The flight from the self can be just as illuminating. Do you agree? Do you think, in your experience with teaching, that is not where people usually start out?

SF: I think motherhood and poetry do meet, unavoidably, at least for me, but perhaps it took a long while for them to do so. (And I admit that I do nurture a faith in the maternality of the universe—I'm glad it surfaces in the poems.) At the same time, I have been more frequently distracted from poetry by motherhood than vice versa, whether it's an emotional or physical, or social even, distraction. Guilt, for example, gets in the way of writing. Or worry! My poetry has been interested in my motherhood, on occasion, and mostly abstractly I guess, in the same way that I am interested in birth and pregnancy as a person, which is why I'm a doula, and it spills into my poetics; or it could be that I forged the two (motherhood/poetry) during a time in my life when I simply couldn't afford to separate them. I think being a mother has allowed me to expect more from my poems, actually, while also feeling more compassion towards them, if that makes sense. Or maybe I'm more patient, much more patient with my writing than I was before becoming a mother. Even as a young mother, when Nora was a baby, I had so much less time to spare, I didn't feel that I could always afford to wait. Now, it could be that I wait too long! But in the end, as you say, it grows tiresome to talk about. Whether or not my poetry is influenced by my being a mother, or vice versa, seems not as interesting as exploring and intuiting my actual process as its own unique phenomenon.

In answer to your question about whether one ought to expect poetry to uncover something about the self: I do agree with you that the flight from the self can/does illuminate—the "Field Notes" poems, and others in my book, mean to address just this idea. I find, for myself, that until I have some distance—from my emotional present—I can't get into the language I need to make a poem. When I teach poetry, I find without fail that students, of any age, have the most success with writing generated out of language and chance, rather than writing generated out of specific life experience (a topic, a narrative). These experiences get sorted out one way or another in our poetry anyway, I think, because language is something that is alive and that we live through, that shapes *everything* about being human. The poem itself is the experience, or should be.

For me, the joy in writing poetry comes from immersing my-self in the language of the poem, hearing it and playing with it and building it, shaping it on the page or in my mouth, allowing the lan-guage that arrives to decide "what the poem is about." I sense this joy in your writing and it's what I love best about *Starred Wire*—which is why it was especially rewarding to *hear* you read those poems. You gave each poem exactly its sound in your voice, and the way you relished each word—and its context—delivered whorls and layers of new pleasures!

When we met, we talked for a minute about what happened to you (and seems to be happening to me now) when *Matinees* was in production and about to be released. This experience of feeling dis-oriented, or lost from the work in a sense. You said, and it is *precisely* how I feel, that it was almost as if you had to "rebuild" yourself from the bottom up, as a poet. I mentioned that while my book has been in production, I seem to be undergoing a fairly significant aesthetic change, which makes editing kind of a struggle! I wonder if you feel that you underwent a significant aesthetic change between *Matinees* and *Starred Wire*. I imagine being in Morocco must have redirected you aesthetically in some ways. But I find the two books to be quite different, even though obviously written by the same poet. *Matinees* seems to have a more rambling, Frank O'Hara style, maybe a bit more casual and youthful, whereas *Starred Wire* feels, to me, elegant, cosmopolitan, exact. I like them both a great deal, and find that what

I like about one is very different from what I like about the other. What do you think? When you came back to a sense of belonging in your work, after the first book, did you find yourself writing very different kinds of poems? What did the first book teach you about your future work?

AM: I was nodding throughout your post. The question of crisis and aesthetic change and the five years between *Matinees* and *Starred Wire* are hard for me to tackle. To paraphrase Godel's paradox: Can any self-description be both honest and complete? For a while I had two distinct problems:

1. I moved to New York, and then
2. I left New York.

I came back to New York after almost a year in Morocco. Well, this was a bit of overload. Most of my twenties had been spent in New England, drifting from job to job and apartment to apartment, writing on my own then going to grad school. That, in a word, was *Matinees*. Then I found myself in a global capital, where the first thing on the morning news was the Dow Jones Industrial Average. Then I ended up in the mountains of Morocco. And making trips all over Morocco and a few forays into Europe. How could I process this? And what on earth did it have to do with everything I had learned about writing up till then—the "make it new" requirement, for instance: How to describe what I was seeing and "make it new?" How to incorporate the extraordinary stories I was privy to and "make it new?" How to "make it new" in the wake of not only my favorite (New York School) poets, but the wake of Language Poets, whom my friends and sharpest critics in New York contended with and made me contend with? What about the problem of translation—do I tell my Moroccan friend, whose struggle in life was to reconcile the philosophical values he had imbibed at the Sorbonne with the fact of intellectual repression in Morocco, do I tell this friend that I write "experimental poetry?" What does it mean? Am I just being frivolous? These were questions that reading Raymond Roussel and Kenneth Koch couldn't answer.

(Kenneth Koch, upon finding out that I was going to live in Morocco, sent a gift my way through Jordan Davis: a signed copy of *On the Edge*. And though I adore those African poems, no way could I reproduce that tone of wonder and ebullience. It was not wonder and ebullience I felt. I was in cultural crisis; I was losing the innocence that allowed me to speak so freely and confidently in my youth; I could no longer take anything for granted.)

Was I frivolous? When I came back to New York everything seemed frivolous. Then there was September 11, and the irony of my husband having worked there, as a paralegal in the North Tower, and it was that job he quit in order to take the one in Morocco. And all of this was snowballing into the feeling that I had experienced important things, so I must have important things to say, that's what poets do. But no, that's not really what I want poetry to do—I am not going to be a spokeswoman or a social or moral critic. I still believe that the ending of "Ode to Michael Goldberg(' s Birth and Other Births)" is worth fighting to write, or I'm fighting for the right to write it against the Spectacle, even the Spectacle of global emergencies.

This is an account of what happened between those books. I feel tender now toward *Matinees*, which I had put aside for a while. I feel those poems are a testament to youth, they have integrity, and most importantly to me, it evinced all those O'Hara-ish qualities you mentioned before they became—just a couple years later—a trend.

SF: I reread your email yesterday and, like the first time I read it, feel that I have so much to respond to. Like you said, this writing about poetry is so distracting from the writing of poetry itself, and lately I have been really caught up in this writing about it.

I also want to mention that just in the past couple of weeks, a depression finally lifted which touched down this summer and was pretty severe. While it isn't literally another country, depression is a foreign and a demanding location, and in it my survival skills—among them writing poems—seem utterly useless, even frivolous. Depression, unfortunately, is something I've had to contend with for most of my life. I know poems indeed come out of it, but only in its aftermath. I had a miscarriage in August, and in addition to that I had really become worn down by the incredible and horrifying choices being made on our behalf by the current administration. We're in such a dark time. What place has poetry in all of this?

In my teaching, I work with many marginalized communities and in the meanwhile, I'm extending my own aesthetic into territories these communities would have no interest in or use for. As you recall, how to "make it new" while also addressing the dilemmas of class and race divisions I encounter every day; to make a poetry both utilitarian and artful—an overwhelming task. When I ease back into the comfort zone of stylistic play or poetic inquiry, I almost feel guilty, maybe even lazy. I think I do expect poetry to address these important things, and I don't think I've quite figured out—from a new awareness—how to make that happen within the aesthetic leaps my poetry wants to take now. I also know that poetry will locate its own language, if I can tune in to it rather than demand it to "say something." Like you, I believe that a poem like "Ode to Michael Goldberg('s Birth and Other Births)" is worth fighting for, is revolutionary. Is it selfish to focus most of my energies on an activity that matters to so few? I think instead it's the job I have, and it's my responsibility to fight for it regardless of the contradictions I face.

Another issue for me at the moment is that I've started a new manuscript—*The Brain Letters*—and my vision of it has seemingly eclipsed my capacity to write it. Am I setting myself up? Or fearing the challenge of embarking upon such an experimental project (possibly alienating even more readers)? Or eliminating the possibility for new poems that fall out of the project's range? It's been hard to focus on something new with the first book about to come out, and those poems already feel like they were written by someone else! I'm definitely in flux, but lately, at least, I have confidence that the next wave of poetry is coming towards me, and that I'm ready to catch it.

This, in brief, touches on my own crisis. Like you, I do not want to be a spokeswoman. I just want to write poems, and to trust that it isn't in vain.

AM: We both can honestly say that self-interrogation about our art—even through the gentle prodding of a sympathetic colleague—is grueling.

I am really sympathetic to what you say about wanting poetry to be able to address our dark time, to address the families you work with.

The only contemporary poetry book that makes me rethink my own poetics in light of its successful political storytelling is Anne Winters's *The Displaced of Capital*. Her technique is about as far from ours as it gets. It is a rebuke to a generation of avant-garde theorists that claimed poetry can only be political by formally mirroring systemic (translated to syntactic) change. Her narrative poem "An Immigrant Woman" is as detailed and involving as a novel (in it, a child is killed in an illegal tenement by city negligence). "The Mill-Race" is an almost biblical description of workers at rush hour in Lower Manhattan. "The Displaced of Capital" takes into account the mass migration of third-world workers to New York. Really, these three poems alone are a rebuke to New York poets; they seize the brutal contemporary moment.

My agony about the state of the world is not political, not alleviated by theories about poverty and ignorance and the hope of progressivism; it is theological, it is theodicean, and if my poetry encodes this at all, it will emerge as a spiritual theme and not a polemic. It emerges slantwise, and it emerges incompletely and unsatisfactorily.

But maybe poetry, for me, is the child itself? Beautiful and innocent and limited and powerless in the real world? And for all those reasons, essential and essentially lovable; existing only to be loved?

SF: I am preparing for the anxiety which surely will accompany the release of the book, although I sense that I may be past the worst of it, in anticipation. We'll see. I am still having trouble easing into the making of a poem, it's as if I've completely lost my sense of how to begin. Or, that I have nothing worthwhile to say. Last night I was pondering this, trying to write, coming up with a few lines that seemed merely clever, and realizing that at least for now I have no interest in style whatsoever. Like you, I find myself quite unable to succeed at narrative description in poetry, though I too have tried, and I suppose several years ago it may have even been a primary mode for me. At the same time, I'm not sure that's the way I really want my poetry to go, or that I enjoy such poetry so much anymore. I've been rereading Virginia Woolf's diary the last few days, and aside from appreciating the pure pleasure and sharpness of her prose, I'm noting how very different my own approach to a "diary" or notebook is, so unlike a fiction writer—I rarely feel compelled to go too deeply into character analysis (aside from my own!) or narrative descriptions—I am less interested in stories and sentences than I am in words themselves, what they really mean, how they sound, their associations. I guess what I'm saying, in agreement generally with what you've said, is that I do admire Anne Winters's *The Displaced of Capital*, but I think it's more of a rebuke to society than to specific poets (though that sentiment probably can't be avoided.) And I wonder too how many people have actually read Winters's work, could its print run even come close to a mass-market crime novel, for example, that practically sanctions everything Winters rebukes? As a writer, an apprentice, the poetry I'm interested in reading and writing usually takes a much more lyric approach. Therein, though, lies the dilemma, with how to say "something meaningful" in almost a foreign language, or at least a tone that is entirely unfamiliar and alien to the masses. It seems to me that some poets are able to accommodate lyricism and a kind of generosity, openness, very well—in particular the New York School poets, like Koch, Edwin Denby (a recent discovery!), O'Hara.... Thus we love them.

What you say about your agony—your call to articulate—being not political or theoretical but theological—I really couldn't have said it better myself, and agree with you utterly. There is a language in between thought and narrative, and that is the language of poetry for me, and is what I aim for; whether it's ultimately a gamble, I guess I've chosen to follow through. Like you said towards the beginning of this interview, I can't *make* people care about poetry just as my poetry can't *make* people care about political corruption and social injustice. I guess that's part of the gamble, to keep trying anyway.

I wanted to talk about particular poems in *Starred Wire*. I think one of my favorite poems is "The Flowers Grow Out of the Cracks in the Stacks"—like many of your poems, there's this underlying sense of play, but also of radically transforming landscapes. The library, "safe within a general surround of Realism" (as you write in "Femme Fatale Geography"), very soon becomes something not quite a library—or greater than a library—viewed through a poetic Eye who can envision an "afterlife of forests." I wonder if you could talk about your sense of play and pun in poetry, and how the image works as portal to inventing a playful or unexpected atmosphere for the poem.

AM: I think the sense of play comes as much out of logical play as images. Have you ever read Lewis Carroll's "Sorites," his nonsense syllogisms? It's perfect that the author of the consummate children's book was primarily a mathematician. Finding the absurdity in logic is akin to finding beauty in absurdity. Which leads back to dreams, childhood, first books. The world was rich and strange once, despite what the newspapers drill into us.

This is a good segue to a question I've been meaning to ask you: what exactly do you mean when you say in your author's statement that the parts of *Because Why* describe The Fool's journey? This is a two-part question because I want to have a clearer understanding of the parts (I thought the book would function just as well as a seamless whole), but I am also intrigued by your use of the archetype. Maybe I just have a one-track mind these days, but I felt like your persona evokes The Child much more than The Fool, which to me seems like a trickster. I don't sense a trickster at all in your work. There is a mystical sense of trust and sincere bewilderment. Most of all, there is hope.

I think also of your e.e. cummings epigraph: he is the Child or Fool of the Modernists, and you follow him in upending the linearity of the line (leapfrogging adjectives and nouns and verbs, for instance) and in the childlike insistence on adjectives and adverbs. (Childlike, of course, carries no stigma in my mind.) The poems still maintain shapes and contours and closures, which is satisfying on the most basic level—that is to say, you don't try to challenge the basic notion of a poem/song/lyric even though you do disrupt syntax. Okay, this is a longwinded question, but you see what I'm getting at. So tell me about the Fool?

SF: Lewis Carroll seems a perfect example for your sense of play as you describe it here—and yes, logical play. Clearly I share your admiration for childhood and its perspective of the world—its rich strangeness. My concept of the Fool as it pertains to *Because Why* is much more akin to the Child than to the Trickster—in fact I think for me Fool and Child are almost synonymous, if the Fool perhaps has evolved through cynicism where the Child has yet to encounter it. The Trickster, as an archetype, does seem to have a leading role in much contemporary poetry—seems to me the Trickster is very interested in irony, parody, and a more coded language. My poems have not embraced this role, and I see the Trickster as being almost opposite to the Fool. I guess I really want poetry to be generous; maybe I keep coming back to this point by circumnavigating it. The Child or Fool is generous in that he/she is all wonder, questioning: tabula rasa. He/she is at zero, and in a sense is kind of liberated by not having to know. I don't see *Because Why* as being in parts per se—I mean I do see it as being a whole. I think my primary reason for *sectioning* the book as I did is that I wanted there to be breathing room for the reader, I wanted there to be friendly bits so that the book didn't feel intimidating, without break. I know that many of my poems are dense, and long, and I wanted there to be a sense of order I guess and of spaciousness. Also, though, I was thinking of Dante, in terms of a kind of "Fool's Journey"—though my Fool and her journey are of course on a different scale and she travels in very different realms. I also think of the number ten as being such a number of completion—for the child, for example, when learning his numbers, when he gets to ten it's a grand accomplishment, like a closure. I liked there being nine, for all kinds of intuitive reasons that I can't quite explain. I see each section as being a kind of cycle the speaker(s) goes through, so that each section is self-enclosed in a way, but also has its own specific task. I'm reluctant to break it down too much, or to predetermine anybody's reading of it. But I guess I think of the sections as being little errands that catapult the speaker into new realms of questioning—maybe each section is like a reduction more than an accumulation. I think of them, at their most simple, as being little realms, little villages that must be passed through on the journey, each with a conflict or confusion to be translated and resolved in a way—maybe like Psyche's tasks, that might be an analogy. If anything, the first poem (all imperatives) is a kind of launching pad into something far less "certain." I do come to poetry in a state of bewilderment, every time. I wonder if this is part of my block—I'm not approaching it this way. I wonder if this business with the book has something to do with feeling as though I need to be *less* bewildered, somehow in control? There's certainly a gap, between the business part of it (books, mags, peers, etc.) and the process itself. Almost like a loss of innocence?

Well. I so much enjoy *Starred Wire,* I think precisely because I can hear the child in the poems, and I feel I can follow her wild perceptions, while simultaneously enjoying the gorgeous, elegant language of the poet through whom this child speaks. And really, it's not at all a somber book, I think it's overwhelmingly a joyful book, and this, for me, seems a completely apt response to any form of violence in the world. Did you ever read the book, as a child, *The Country Bunny?* It's really a fabulous book, about a mother bunny (single mom!) who has twenty-three children, a very humble plain-looking bunny, and who wants to be the Easter Bunny. In order to facilitate this ambition, to prove to the old Grandfather of the Easter Bunnies that her household will buzz along without her, she has trained her twenty-three children to fulfill the important roles in her absence. At least half of the children have jobs involving the arts—some paint, some dance and sing, and some write stories and poems. Because the necessity for pleasure as vital—if not more so—to the well-being of the household as are the jobs like dishwashing and bill-keeping. So, in my mind, you've done the world a great service with your poems, and I hope you rest easy with this, and keep writing them!

SARAH FOX

A Concept of Zero

I.

Some One awakens

      someOne a weight absconded
          from possible dream
               or flung through star crowds   (*sleeping*)

to "awaken" flat on an archaic stone step
      at the foot of the Pantheon
                  Every shard of language
—Italian, Japanese, Swiss (?)—
          hovers, friendless—nest of bees

Awake where Rome is

                  city of Zero   the dead

      god(s) sleeping in the stones of their ruin   —
          dome-shaped dreams unravel narratives

behind frescoes, hallucinating stone   —
          behind the deafness of language

One awakens to a humming cavity of human sound heard through a deafness

the weight of intonation—Moroccan, Estonian, German (?)—a *POW* in the
                        heartbeat's murmur

      One on a stone as if inside a hive—

      the Pantheon admiring clouds through its rooftop eye

A child's plaster hand among the rubbish

Downards One hears water hauled through ducts—
        underground arteries where dead god(s) dream

The hive-shaped talking heard through a stone—Papal, romantic, obsolete—

Water water water mulching the logic of ruin

                as if whispering something like *Appia*   *Aqua*

Balloon-headed children flock the fountain

      nod off their shudder like a headache, coin toss

        Here where Rome is   is breathless?

As if the stone's rink were a flame
      of sound in the distance
As if the deaf stone had begun to melt,
        One urged through its skin   something

        like a
            diving

                    Ciao

2.

She elects

        descent   (underground?)

            flying-like resuming gills

like aqueductriverbank,

         unfolding among god(s) and ruin groves
     something happens

Sound   —   detached   —   roams
    the cloud within O
         of arched and uncoiling brain
intervening
      with
             a sleep

Swan-god sleep—long-
        necked
    and diving

It is like an actual
    dive,
being put to sleep emulating
river-river-river-river-river-river-river-duct   :

     "a body enters the water"   :

      stone's rink of flame
      minus cloud   (*child's hand-shell, dropped*)
      swan unfolding, glistening

Prayer migrates from "*I think so*"   (I   *say*   so)
    into "make love"   (*make me*)

3.

                    ... an eggshell halved and dripping on the bank
                                                        ... swan
        One, from an O

A fish jumps: water circles out to the limit of sound
Vibrations of fish thought in the absence of fish

                The farther the circle the larger the thought?

    Thought of fish-who-failed-to-fly at the tenth circle of being alive

                Swan: spherical and in-the-middle
                                        a prayer, at zero

        "Pain is four-dimensional and subjective"   "Change is painful"

At ten in the district of pain
                            life appears absent at the limit of thought

On the tenth day of the month I left the body of my mother
When my body grows to ten a birth is immanent

The baby, sludging through its duct
                            A new hand sprung at the root of
                                            her reaching

        Water: the baby falling out with the sea
And the smell of the sea
                        what was in me: baby, sea:
                            what has left me: baby, sea

                        The baby plunges through zero

The body dives through a thought made by a fish

                                    entering prayer again
                                    Prayer = "entering into"
                                                (me + zero = swan)

Unfolding wing to wing   —   again, then again

then

Owl (from *The Brain Letters*)

At the peak of shine, a slope without sleeve.
Nexus of the snowy Himalayas.
Fixed in its bony socket, the great unmoving eye
of you, Dear Owl: of Owl am me.
Owl a yellow saucer in the dark conical thicket.
Inner orb on a peak and distant, darting.
My rickety eye molting in Owl's plundered nest of me.

Mobbing birds pester Owl.
Screeching birds, all kinds of wildlife—
garrulous, tawdry, maculate—thought-beast
canopy between us. Only
the thought of dark is dark.
The thought of forest is any forest,
thought-forest noising up the trees.
And distantly earless Owl talk, even what sounds
like the soft cooing of a dove in the forest.
You have the face of the earth and so it belongs to you.
Disk-faced, reflective, Owl's eyes
are larger than the brain.
The blink of Owl is a third eyelid
made of see-through skin; Owl's
third eye an ambit in the rotary
dizziness of Nobody.

It is still winter and it is always winter
and the owlets are likely to crash land.
If S is forest floor that sees through herself
then Owl is that surveyor of its own wasted
progeny, cloud orbiting the hemisphere.
What it sees ends in what it sees.
Aloof hero in the dwelling of self.

From an emptiness the point of vision
is a plain thing, desire in absentia from its form.

Dear Owl, romancing the common chapel
at the edge of space. Dear question,
credible to clouds. The alchemy of Owl
is its own private mind: mind within
the mind's nocturnal hallucination
like a difficult promise nudging the membrane
of being. Being not-Owl, being bepetaled owl talk
wakening, wakening, wings nailed to a bark.
Fixed on a balcony magnificently speechless,
robed like the snowy Himalayas
pointing their way to God in the unaccomplished
light of living creatures. Neither mother nor
father, neither circumference nor migration.

Elsewhere lives an owl in an elsewhere tree.
Seen through S, it is still winter.
Owl finds nothing useful. Owl's
eyeballs do not move around. Perched
yellow saucer in the methodical
dark. Owl eternally abroad
and at ease. Is Owl? Is Owl not?

The owl, of course, is neither 'good' nor 'bad.'
The owl is just an owl.

Dear S (from *The Brain Letters*)

Drug through the slow gut
    of my own flame,
<down>   <downwards>   I,
    worm-wet, shady, buried am.
Too obedient to burn

We can invent language
    every time: one
syllable and
    then
another—*the swift composure of a fish*

What is pain?
   Inevitable
What is suffering?
   Not
"Reports of pain will be believed
    Controlling your pain may speed your recovery"

Beyond the room's ceiling
    fan, whipping,
another patient shrieks
    in a pen
The hourly flashlight arrives without knocking.
    Can't you give him the medicine?
"That freak is a criminal"

    I hear him scream himself a new body,
rough flesh disgorging from the animal stone

My dream-houses are always hospitals
    Wards and halls and white
a bright fear, lockdown, hovering—
    the medicine's lumber in upset

I begin to recall
    the last time I felt

the lithium in my brain
   An elemental event,
some peculiar brand
   of attention—is it really real,
in me?

"The only way to get an accurate
   diagnosis is to have a *complete*
physical and mental examination"

The lithium moves
   at the speed of trees,
inevitably
   A dull moth pegged to a screen,
stray eye under the bed

By evening's end the brain
   whips its metallic synaethesia
against my skull
   Above me, verb-headed,
horizons of noise are pursued
   Tears are liquefied brain

You arrive with your two
   hallucinating hands to tell
me "Watch what I can,
   pull out of your mind"—

train, boat, catfish,
   beach ball, wrenches, snowfort,
shipwreck, squirrel, parrot,
   tree stump, vowels, pianos … metal bed …
neon ghosts and clouds:
reeling them out of my head on a skein of air

The cavity swirls into its gulch, swept
   wooden planks, where a girl—"like
a feather"—thinks: "Every once in a while
   I suddenly find myself dancing."

Sarah, What Have You Done?

She imagined a couch—or coral,
her arm slung open to the elements.
Nobody's the boss of her.

It was hard work becoming untangled,
her and Nobody turning each other over.
She said "Look for the red spot

in the center of the room." It was a lie,
though it distracted. In the center
of the room, THE PILLS, and beside them

stood THE PLANT: Get Out Of Jail Free
in an otherwise reliable deck. Between
them, an arm slung open to the elements.

A sweet poison for the age's tooth.
The arm bent at the wrist making a bridge.
Over troubled water it shall sail.

"Sir," she said (or "Honey")
"can you tell me who I am?"
In the house next door Rome fell.

"Like me, you are a piece of clay
dropped in the wilderness." He'd been
noting her, by command of a cloud.

The clouds engulf the horizon. Toward
them people drive their cars over bridges,
first fearing then undergoing panic.

She began, from a lifeboat on the river,
to watch the panic occur to her up there self.
Like experiencing a drive-in, sound muffling in.

Witnessing a movie's murder.
The bridge might slope like a wrist.
It might break open, a eucharist.

There's a rib in her that can only be troubled
by wine. One evening the rib discharges
the rest—(arms, wrist, girth).

Afterwards, having lost her cloud-self,
the rib stands alone: a mainsail. In no time,
pills affix to it. She: this and thus.

Around that rib, the pills spin like gymnasts.
And then a pore opens, green pustule
growing into brain, an actual being.

Lost rib, sloping bridge of wrist, tooth-root.
A crossing over, rib to rib. Just the once.
I haven't done anything at all.

Not Want

Weather stops looking
small or large, cold, decadent.
Chimes in an uproar ebb
into the cardboard horn of a passerby.
To not melt across distances.
To steadily watch and not like
being reached after, being swatted.
Like a cute fly. Liking even sucking
long on a cigarette not today.
To follow the road hand-in-hand with a medicine.
Wow. Exclamations excuse themselves
to the far lots. Subdued. Like having a fever
in a Motel 6, the tube on, the pitiful line-up.
Being made comfortable upon a sameness,
tedious, fingertips, tree-bark.
To be a brain in cahoots with invention.
To be touched, or not touched, indefinitely—
so. To be pressed against a margin
not anchored down or solicitous.
Glum crows eat the many many leftovers.
My body seems to spit its luster back
to the gallows of the earth, some original
luxurious fire gripped by indifference,
below a shadow, pursuing the point, inevitably,
of an elaborate and scalloped numbness
To swallow it anyway.

M: In Memoriam

My so-called desire tows a bird around, she is mute
and spends years nesting, pecking through brick.
She looks more like a pug than a bird.
She's resplendently useless.

My so-called desire tows several empty coats, M—[1],
an imbroglio, "protective" cells that can't stop spinning
into beasts or paperweights. Calculated
merger <cf. *marriage*> always preferable
to surefire anonymity,
even a placid reprieve. The walls in here taste like steel.

                    Occasionally unleashed
like a sheet off a couch, I and my so-called desire
hover quietly side by side and gaze
collectively through a hole in the window.
We make the shape of certain clouds which
on days like this resemble simple-minded dragons
or circus elephants. M—[2] lifts up my skirt

but I've left the room *in a sense* and anyway
                              I'm too marooned.
A noseless cat creeps through the dust carving
ancient principles that don't cohere.
My S.C.D. and I view them upside down
from our stellar height.

Summations and bifocular portals emerge,
predicting that the resistance
of terror and the tiny red onslaught of ants
can be managed for only so long. M—[3] refuses to spontaneously combust.

The bird and I wish hard through the night.
We dream about murders committed conveniently
by strangers. We dream

about houses so vacant the silence elopes
with the memory of a thud mistaken for a knock.

Once I awoke alone on a hinge.
Almost a raft,
abandoned to the possible notion that
it may simply be a matter of shell games.
What are the chances that all this time
we've been shackled to an incorrect moon?

Scopalamine

After a lifetime of living under Catholic occupancy
I went to the Maghreb and met underground philosophers:
"If you can provide secondary source material
proving John Locke had a pessimistic view of human nature
I will give you my car, but if I can provide
secondary source material proving Kant masturbated daily
you have to give me five U.S. dollars."
At the parapet where the drug dealers, all sub-Saharans,
stared fixedly at Iberia, one of the students broke her glasses
and had to go back to Mama and Papa in Marrakesh.
Papa, who was French, would make her pay for them
but it was her love of her literature instructor, who may've been a spy,
that made her sojourn pajama'd into his bourne. He, alas
had an assignation with the hostess from the Hotel Mektoub
and if that fell through, a chemist who analyzed gold.
It was a university of underground drunks,
adding to the exotica of foreign faculty, who already said anything.
"Never once in my country have I taught what I believed!"
snapped a Fassi behind closed curtains, sipping wine.
"Mon jeune ami!" he said sardonically.
"I was punched by guards at the Tunis airport
for saying I was conducting research.
I was accused of Christianity by a student
who spotted a cross in the shield of my Durham
sweatshirt!" A slightly reckless hilarity—
"Of course I am mad, I have studied philosophy.
The rest, who have studied anthropology,
are merely alcoholic." "As when a dream that offers a vision
of one's life restored is not itself a means of restoration,"
I confessed to someone who would promptly decamp,
abandoning her possessions, to Berlin, "I am afraid
I can never write a poem about this, for to write a poem

is to lie, and this is already a country of falsehoods,
where everything is yes; all gesturing nods."

Furthermore, take a town like El-Hajeb, so fresh
with new paint and asphalt because the first El-Hajeb
washed away in a flashflood, though no one read about
the hundreds dead in the newspapers; one day new gutters
appear along the road from the mountains to the Meknes plain.
When the boys, for then there are towns like Asilah,
jump off thirty-foot battlements to the Atlantic Ocean
no boy-dolphin is ever lost. Far from the boy-dolphins
the second El-Hajeb. So far from the second El-Hajeb
the first El-Hajeb, and the one-armed housekeeper
from El-Hajeb: when her employer was found
in the faculty parking lot naked and gibbering
she stood accused of poisoning him with scopalamine,
sold in the souk as a love drug.
Which El-Hajeb had she come from, and where had I arrived,
certainly not Europe, when the ferry landed in Algeciras?
Spain was not Europe in the sense of a second U.S.
or a first U.S., preceding it, of course, and that first night
in Grenada I broke down laughing, led back to the pension
where the cold man at the desk held our key, thinking
the Alhambra has cast a spell, this is the second Africa
and unless a double negative, I must not be the first me.

Coda

First time I saw egrets, cuckoos, kestrels, storks.
Wish I missed it—
the pomegranate library
at Tamagroute; a gate painted all colors. (That
was Ain Leut, cedar village,
gyroscope required in its
mountain streets.)
Near was the source of *source*, violent blue.
What is Magic then? They said Magic
still existed there. I want the Love Potion, I said,
to make life less intermittent.

First jacarandas, oleanders, hibiscuses.
Nightshades.
An antidote, they said, were doorways shaped as keyholes.
Go in through those
and in any *ville*, even *nouvelle*, even
in the arrangement by guilds
of one notorious since the Middle Ages,
all newspapers will be one day old.
First eagle. First carpet of orange poppies.
If I couldn't love first,
how would I find the Love Potion?

Omar

"If you could reach up into any orange tree
and eat when you were hungry—"
São Paolo oranges, to be precise, with leaves like tildes over O's

"—you could pick the egg—" the glossy black egg
with gilt patterns that came from Byzantium via *Moskva*
beside the miniature samovar,

a few pussy willows,
a paddle that when describing a quick circle
caused a passel of hens to peck the paddle;

"—from your Baba's cabinet."
Sunset end of the Umma, and the cloth in Café Tuareg
black with gold designs on which men set

glasses and poured tea from *mosque-high*.

Faeries of the Maghreb: A Ballad

for Steve McNamara

Faeries were prone to kidnap musicians. *Whiskies are beers boiled to
steam, restored to life by condensation.* A vengeful mermaid rose when
men of Leek Firth tried to drain the Black Mere. *Spirits reflect their
place of origin. Sifted through rock, water will taste like iron or Viking blood.
If like snowmelt, then a gift of god.* Banshees followed families with O
or Mac in their names. One might shut a door against them but never
insult; they took words to heart. *Barley was the start of civilization.*
Fairies are older than barley.

When you were delirious with fever in Moulay Bousselham I ran down
to the souk panicked along an esplanade lit with rag-stuffed flaming
butane cans, jostling with donkeys, junksellers, food carts, children,
arguments, courtships, conspiracies, waiters taking orders by the moon
or the neon of *teleboutiques* and *pharmacies*.... Surf crashed, boomboxes
paraded on shoulders broadcast *raita* (used in *ghaoua* and *jilala*) and
shirhat (call and response female and male) not like the Andalusian
wedding songs we'd thrilled to, chalice drum, tambourine, lute and
violin. You heard things through small high window while I torqued
through the beats and choruses, the seasons like sirens and (me in tears
begging) would not drink the water, bottled, I brought.

British explorers recorded dwarflike peoples in the Moroccan
highlands: "Dark-complexioned smiths and magicians" made houses on
irregular axes in the mountains, with gay and irregular patterns. They
may have been the Scottish brownies; they may have built Stonehenge;
they may have migrated north with Phoenicians on ships bearing the
technology of distillation; they may have bred descendants who were
captured by corsairs and spirited back to the Atlas whose inhabitants,
some, have blue eyes to this day.

Anecdote of Girls in the World

Crept, bodices smearing broom,
heather and lichen,
to the drop off the chalk cliff, limestone
still in the interstices

of linens, but they saw the ocean. A satisfying
craquelure develops
from debaucheries across
the Manchurian ice

or through the emerald camera
of a diaphragm
in limestone; across the quetsch clay tripped
by a miffed hoof

or a swamp in Belarus in the shape of a walrus.
"A tune to urge turtles"
nettled by the craquelure keeps the accents in—
a signature develops

when the air's blasted
through a brass J, dirty puff in the subway
forced up from the tunnel
to the platform where the girls

crept up to the edge of the track
and soot still in the interstices
of their bodices
when they went back to their walls, masterpieces.

Orphic Glazier

"A Russian an Italian and an American arrived at a space station …"
"A Mexican band playing reggae in England …" Chauffeur's cellphone
murmurs Urdu. Midsummer. City lights blur like fairy tracers in a forest.

We ascend bridges, titanic string instruments, harps and cellos plucked
in our dreams, in our heavenly heads, in those gray clouds we haul
around in braincases, tipped back on two-wheeled dollies as we roll and
gaze and gaze.

Change of season, heavenly brains discharge our many selves to walk
around old neighborhoods, starry evening, photons raining down
through mesh as one girl passes
beneath graffitied stanchions. Lots hold pit bulls leashed beyond pity,
barking into the sky; bushes flower on their own initiative or don't. She's
saying, Where's this restaurant? Another is on a plane to Morocco.

I dream she has a seating chart for words somewhere, with mysterious
considerations that place bureau next to burr alphabetically, or trophy
& nourishment etymologically, or belligerence & beauty experimentally.
But she is in a foreign country, so making her language foreign to itself
isn't helping anything. It is strange already.

Restaurants are strange too: "If you go to a restaurant, people feel sorry
for you. It means you're away from home." Home: there is another self,
putting her possessions
on the sidewalk, things the movers aren't taking away, and there is the pit
bull barking out back, the runaway roses, trashpickers already circling,
men next door bearing
fresh panes of glass that look like they could burst with the ever
springing car alarms on the industrial boulevard—didn't they used to be
called *glaziers*, as in Cocteau's *Orphée*?
It doesn't say it on their sign. Nor will the shops have glass in the
medinas. In the ville nouvelle, built by the French, yes. Wherever there
will be assigned seats, or long lines,
blame sticks to "French-style bureaucracy," or girls who speak French,

enraging the taxi drivers who rebuke them in Arabic, or women whose bastillas are like their inward pride, butter-cinnamon-sugary, disguised by outward modesty (pastry). "The cuisine is delicious, just find yourself some home cooking." Words nowhere specific as the one for plucking feather by feather birds for the recipe.

And when she sees illicit chickens on rooftops from the bridge ramp, she thinks she understands gibberish: an imaginary sylvan demon, big as a chicken: *ghoul* (from the Arabic) or *ghost* (from the Icelandic), ambushing from the dendrites—because this is the dream still. Blame can be laid on the dream where the seating chart has strange words talking to each other. Language made foreign to itself and identity lost in a dream are pleasurable in the same way, pleasurable most in the moment—*"Here!" I say running to the man carrying the windshield.*—that making—*I hurl a word at him*—wakes sense.—*which shatters it:* glazier.

Atlas

Zsigmond II & Zsigmond III in the Romi-Isetta
up the switchbacks of Santos
in the time of Quadros

pushing when it overheats;
no "differential" III explained, re the back wheels.
Why *this* vision, in a jeep

on hairpins of the Middle Atlas
turns on missing him; or the hashish;
or (but Lacerda was not an assassin)

hearing the CIA
taught Hassan's secret police to dissolve bodies in vats of acid.
Romanov-acid: Code Anastasia.

These Representations of Wartime

The liftoff from a rooftop coop
distant thunder of the icemaker
child in a tenement stairwell
a cement echo in the art deco
shambles: these are not the
terms to discern a sentence by,
except a sentence that wraps
its back in a negative embrace
against you, made a fence.
It is a sentence so philosophical
naturally asymptotic butterflies
agree not to land on definitive
subjects, topiaries.
(Monarch migration season—
a *Lincoln slept here* glamour
to the rose of sharon.)
Urban perennials flare out of lots
in which legs of chairs
suspended in the tangle extrude
hidden toys in the foliage
and last blossoms like teacup sets
smashed til only odd ones left.
When tractor trailers roar past
tripping anti-theft devices
we all cease to speak, honoring
the uncertain fate awaiting things
whose words retain the sound
of verse: victoria, brougham, caleche....
The sky has an ardor for clouds,
avatars of lambs when lambs
populated the vocabulary.
Take the treated flannel cloth
that in jewel blue'll rub the smears
out of the lenses, put on glasses.
Spiderwebs on undersides buttresses.

But now, reader, get ready for
a *real* scene of horror:
There's not a word demanded of you
by all this air and leafery. Not a word.

Microscripts in the Garden

If I mistake the word "evidence" for "violence" briefly,
like a hawk perusing the countryside mistaking

a dachsund for a chipmunk, then I am reading too slowly,
I must read faster and faster! never stopping.

In other words, tired greenery indexed its leaves,
arriving in a sequential data-stream, or data-dream,

clouds positioned hideyholes within abysses,
and what was happening elsewhere changed anyway.

In other words: hot summer day. Photographs
contradicted each other with so much molecular squirming.

So I read faster and faster (how primeval primavera
seemed this year, how far away now) hoping

with more myopia than yoga that my contortions
to get closer and closer to the source text

won't land me in some kind of underground, with the
trees palindrome, with carved initials, dead lovers

reading their own plays backward, over and over.
(Over and over backward plays own their reading.)

Goodbyes

In the harbor breeze concrete playgrounds razor down brown leaves ...
swingsets strops

renovations in medias res go on hiatus ... auto body shops shield
chunky glitter. Livery cabs sans medallions ... sun buttoned up ...

it's not even September empty benches echo laps, mothers' pathos.

    *

Followed in the cemetery! As if a tightly scrolled tongue
made a baton and the words leaped off a boy's shirt,
as he went by with his grandmother ... "Mañana Albania,"
it said, I thought. The baton replied "Boca Raton, Brooklyn
... the botanica segued into restaurant
where what bloomed in the sangrias, like aperçus in papercuts ...
were tiny historical movements ... mass migrations ... andante ..."

Sirens circumscribed a dotted line around the precinct.

    *

Mare's tails predominate ... cirrocumulus x-rays

and the sundressed playground writes in red bars, blue bars, green bars
the rudiments of discipline smothered in sky, showing the grain
of the earth's rotation even in the riverine interstate
pouring through the chainlink hexagons of the overpass ...

The atmosphere's drag in the cursive *Yours*, ...

The Answer Man

I'd stored some vital information in my brain
but access was denied.
I need a crowbar.
Look out, it's gonna be messy.
Just the roof bill alone ...
I'm not saying I haven't been broken into before.
Nor that your own spackling problems are insignificant.
You left a valium on the carseat.
You too will be an ancient child
but now you are a grade school teacher with a great ass
wasted on grade schoolers.
Would that the school burn down down down
so out you'd run, arms in the air,
breasts shouting Fire! Fire!
the wee tykes covered with erasure dust
set free to torture the weakest as is nature's plan.
Then it starts to snow.
Snow likes to pretend it's not going to kill us
like a murderer who comes into a photo shop
to get some film developed only he doesn't have any film.
This happened to Grace who worked there,
who too had spectacular sexual characteristics
she'd allow shaken by power mowers.
He left them when a couple came in with a cracked lens.
Definitely something wrong with this guy, she thought,
what kind of idiot comes to develop film without any film?
The next day the cops came with the answer
but it was one of those answers that only makes more questions
until you realize you've spent half a life in the wrong research wing.
Help! Help! a guy turning green blocking the exit aisle
and you're an expert in butterfly migration.
Oh well, you still find death attractive

in a sister-of-the-bride-Virginia-Woolf way,
its rolled architectural plans,
those death alluding pebbles in the sand
the sea keeps neurotically washing.
Later Death will arrive in a black motorcycle helmet.
He will give us one last piece of cake.

Stoop

What happened had yet to happen,
the trivial tumult everafter,
split-hearted ransacking for cause
and proof, the likelihood that never,
cicada note sustained then frost
full stop. The usual figures limned in,
the angel not yet auditioned, the one
with the bow metamorphed to a stone,
landscape's last laugh, the clouds not yet
in on it, still confident they can unveil
a sun. Nothing moves except time
which means everything moves, a mountain
wiped out by an armada, the armada
wiped out by a rag soaked in linseed oil.
We are all wiped out by a rag soaked
in linseed oil then redone, a hitch
to the side, smaller or larger, only one
original limb left. Sometimes you can feel it
burning, spot weld, dream voltive,
something that never belonged to you,
something you stole, ducking into the dark
until they gave up, gave out into the green
aorta of summer, winter's glass eye,
buried there and now trying to be found,
to be absolved or condemned, peregrine.

Hey Baby

You had reached into a dark hole
but the theogony was gone. Then
there was a shout and the movie broke.
Only the robot monkeys could move
and they had only a couple hours left
in their batteries, the same current event
had been running for years, exchequers
prowling in assault vehicles looking for
just the sort of person to beat the shit out of
I was but no way was I doing their job
for them, least not so you could tell
from my dental records. I controlled myself
on remote. I had a free sub coming.
I wasn't interested in the movie
but the dark was proving exceptional
except for the clichéd screaming.
I longed for my garage. The rag
with its face pushed in many accidents,
the bicycle hung upside down like an attempt
to rehabilitate an instrument of torture,
the interior decoration by bats.
When I'm dead I'll reach up and pull
an attractive lady down by her legs
into my pupa and make a baby.
Baby will build me a monument
and not just some pile of junk either.
Small, inexpensive replicas will be available
in the battlefield gift shop.

Lives of the Primitives

Shouldn't someone have run for help by now?
When I was a child, someone was always running for help.
None returned
but I still like to think of them snookered in phlox,
sucking a hooka, getting the low down from the giant worm.
Everyone was wiser then, no one was excluded
except those who disqualified themselves
by being poor and dirty, not speaking proper English,
low scores, fidgeting during naptime, the deranged.
I knew I was one of them
or would be soon enough
once my sinecure gave out
and I'd crash among pickpockets and divorcees,
dictionary readers, addicts of the instant,
kids with stigmata and spectacular tits,
intemperate artistic folk
counterfeiting wounds for a public
that could never hurt enough.
Obviously I'm damaged goods,
even in my three piece some dictum
from the ant world eats at my nonchalance.
Sure I'd left some broken hearts behind
I don't mind saying and won't be getting
any refunds soon. A new pod of recruits
paces off a wrestling rink, Harvard is in the air
but I think back to what Chow Fat said
as we tearfully parted, socked silly with sake.
It's private but on one level it concerned
the noble perils of adopting a rescue dog
and on another the path to enlightenment
which was true of everything Fat chewed over,
he has a thing for dogs with mean streaks
afraid of their own paws and struck most people
as a drunk faker nitwit which was only half true.
There's so much we still don't know:

the life expectancy of a squirrel, the lair
of the giant squid, the monetary systems
of all those vanished tribes. How strange
to be among westerners again, no longer
handcuffed and strapped in plastic in the driving snows
of the second higher pass, a failed performance
I admit, not like my pal who painted everything
he painted red, red of swallowed shout,
red of pig's snout, he had some kind of argument
then really raked it in. Funny to read
what they write about him now
as if the whole thing wasn't an accident,
the radio on comic opera, the sewage
singing to the sea, the sea swinging back,
as if he wasn't someone who loved a joke
especially on himself.

To the Woman, Not Trying to Fly, Who Fell with Her Legs Closed, Arms Pressed against the Front of Her Body, while Primly Clutching Her Purse

September 11, 2001

I.

You didn't topple, cartwheel or plummet. You believed
that your descent, while swift, would end tenderly,
and that there would then be things to attend to.
While others fell past you, screeching for mercy
and splayed like stars, you aimed your pinpoint of body
towards a future that included checkbooks,
snapshots of squirming children,
a scarlet stump of lipstick.
There would be need for these things again.
Your keenly ordered mind couldn't help but see the vertical
drop as mere inconvenience. You didn't hurtle, flail or pinwheel.
Your eyes straight ahead, your sweet drumming heart
struggling toward a fuss, you were most concerned with decorum,
the proper way for a lady to manage adversity. I watch your fall
and ready myself, for I have been called a lady too.
I will be here to help you to your feet,
to brush strands of the sky from your eyes.

II.

For poets, these are difficult days.
We have at our disposal every letter of every syllable
of every word ever written or spoken in any language,
but when I attempt to bellow the word *fly*, I discover
that it can no longer conjure sound.
There's the man with his skin fused to his shirt.

Perhaps he can tell us why.
There are hands, shoes, cell phones, sudden gifts
in the grit and rubble. Maybe they hold a clue.
There is that blue Toyota Camry sitting for nine days
in the train station lot in Tarrytown, there is *have you*
seen him her them he was she is brown eyes limp tattoo,
there are those thousands of mothers suddenly convinced
that their children had learned to *(fly),*
and chose that one fierce moment
to do so

III.

My granddaughter is obsessed with the drawing of stars.
Each point must be perfect, meticulously measured,
twinkling beyond all reason. We have experimented
with the most efficient ways to manufacture whole
crayoned parades of starlight. We fill entire pages with
nighttime skies where no fiery wink is allowed to flaw.
"Why are you so worried about how the stars look?" I ask.
Grandmaaaa, she says, in that slow exasperated whine
that makes me feel feeble and clueless and utterly loved,
A star has got to be perfect
before God lets it fall.

Waiting for a Title in German

Bitterfeld, Leipzig, Landsberg. On the staticky
radio, an American Negro is marching to Zion.
Neely screeches *sheep!* as the wool blitzes by.
Luis is at the wheel, all gritted molars, sweaty
palms and musical Mexican expletives. None
of us dares look directly at the speedometer,
but with the window rolled halfway down, we
spit hurtled gnats from the surface of our teeth.
The Autobahn has refused to know us, won't
ease roar and wind to fold us in, so we chatter
Our Fathers and notice, for the third time, that
the seatbelts are busted. *If we hit anything, we
die,* Luis observes—no concussions, no slivers
of glass in the eye, no slow-motion rollovers. At
this speed, we would be extinguished, our bodies
would be red mist and smoke. We wonder aloud
at our own obituaries, shamed by the tiny blips
we'd leave behind—notebooks of indecipherable
stanzas, self-published tomes, blurry VHS tapes
of ourselves reading to ourselves. Fighting for a
clear signal on the one station we sometimes
understand, we cheer as Sam Cooke twists his
plaintive tenor to beg Jesus for several favors.
We'll just get in line behind him. Dominique,
drunk on warm wine, hefts an empty, belches
fragrantly, asks if that's Austria we just passed.

Always Hungry

Obscene enticement, the entire head of a hog in
the window of the meat market is fly-speckled
testament to what man will gobble if it can be
bought one quarter at a time. Mama and I will
make sandwiches of this pig's jellied noggin,
slicing the cheese of it thin, drenching snowy
bread with Tabasco. It is this way with us, girls
of the first wave. We crave chicken necks, salt
pork, the pickled feet of pigs. We pluck hairs
from the skin of our suppers, treasure sizzling
drippings in sinkside jars, sop up what's left
with biscuits. Outside of us, cities are torched.
Policies decide who we are, where we will live.
But our souls are hastily crafted of fat, salt
and sugar, all that Dixie dirt binding us whole.

Almost

For Cindy Sheehan

You almost had me. I had written the first line of this poem,
and it was threaded with your son's blood, with the fading
gristle of him, tarnished medals swung from my verbs.
I was almost at your side, both of us violently barren
of boys, mine sucked into the carnage of G swagger,
yours romanced and betrayed by a soft man of murders.
I watched the skewed jazz of your standing and falling,
I listened to the bone scrap of knees and spirit, heard
the definite closing and weeping of your womb. You said,
aloud and aloud, *My son is your news, his huge absence
is your sleep.* Do you remember the newborn Casey,

wailing, silver slick, breaking open your body, insisting
upon the world? What you gave him was the sugared shit
of passage, stickball and skinned joints, a cock flailing
with heat and questions, bud-breasted girls with answers.
You fed him sandwiches of mayo squashed between
sweating slices of the whitest bread, you held a chubbed
hand and led him toward some version of the cross
and patiently you showed him what his knees were for.
Once he found them both, he crawled toward war.

Hours later, Casey was the catch in our throat.
With a single wail, you hard-birthed another child,
a monstrous clump of bones and shadow. You buried
a sweaty t-shirt, a boy, a failed science class, a kiss.

And turned toward your son's killer. Sun-scarred
and patient, you marred his landscape and ached
us all in your role as woman who is left behind.
And you almost had my bullets, my money,
my broken but breathing son as offering. I almost
donned your logo, adopted the face of your minus,

pinned a poster of your quest to my bare skin.
I practiced my mouth around *Casey, Casey,* until
I could rock with the exploding and ride a piece
of Humvee into a hellish void, until the huge hollow
came, bottomless and singular, as stark as thunder.
I was close to forging our link—the hopeful violence
of a birth that comes to nothing, nothing at all.

You said *I wanna give a shoutout to my peeps
in Crawford,* you freckled and chaos-coifed and
unbridled grin, on one of the networks you had
coaxed into line, you said *I wanna give a shoutout
to my peeps in Crawford—and who says we can't
be gangsta?* And I envy and abhor such humor
so close to the gallows, so inside the shuttered
eyes of your gone son. You almost had me in your
clutches, hero, artist's rendering, chapped goddess.
I was yours until you diluted your blood for a sweet
snippet of airtime, before you went so gleefully
and wrongly OG, before the Post snapped you in
a fervent hug, your left hand trapped in the kitchen
of Al Sharpton's hair. Overtoothed, manicured
and professionally emptied, you had moved
beyond mother to become another war, the one
we were sure to win, and have already lost.

I was right there, weary mama alongside your public
revolution, we who have surrendered our sons
to parallel battles. And I am right here, waiting
for you to remember how you lost yours, his chunky
body swirling into pink mist, the sand obscened,
littered with lost muscle and his last known sound,
which, despite your dreams, was not repeated,
was not your name.

speculum oris

*The Speculum Oris was a scissor-shaped instrument inserted into the mouth
of a slave to force the jaws open. The crew of slave ships would force captive
Africans to eat so that they couldn't escape servitude by starving themselves
to death.*

the requisite tunnel
teeth in the way, tapped out
of the wailing
circle
oris
the weeping horn
iron hammered thin
stretches face bone to bend
tongue flails
signs *scream*
in this cave of stunned
speech
rusted screw pierced cheek
twist, tighten,
gums stretched bloodless
speculum
fat flies, not believing
their bounty, explore
dizzied by whispers
of oat rice threads of fat
woe is
snap shut
all thoughts of swallow
snaking head of possible
in the throat
you will eat. you will
live. *eat.* knees scissor
and knock no
to warm water, shredded
meat

last tooth leans, relents
skin welds
around this
iron becomes this
skin
around this iron
becomes this
skin

RAYMOND QUENEAU

from French by Daniela Hurezanu & Stephen Kessler

The Dogs of Asnières

Dogs get buried and so do cats
horses get buried and so do men
hope gets buried and so does life
love gets buried—loves
loves get buried—love
silence gets buried in silence
peace gets buried—peace
peace—the deepest peace
under a layer of colorful pebbles
scallops and colorful flowers

there's a grave waiting for everything
if you wait long enough
night falls day dawns
if you wait long enough
the Seine flows down to the sea
the island stays where it is
the Seine will go back to its source
if you wait long enough

and the island will sail toward the Harbor of Grace
if you wait long enough

dogs get buried and so do cats
two species that don't get along

Vigil

If the lights in the night made explicit signs
fear would be laughter and anguish forgiveness
but for the guard on edge in the cold
the lights in the night are unsettling lines

Harbor

The lengthening wall
the roofs as they fall
the wood all rotten
are all but forgotten

the dangling rigs
the barrels the pigs
gone as they are
aren't really so far

This ship without grace
disappears in space
unmoored the gray day
sails slowly away

Calm is the tree standing straight or twisted
Calm too is the bush in its mediocrity
Calm is the proud horse untouched by froth
Calm is the mushroom and its wife the moss
Calm is the little spring calm the torrent too
Calm is the set course removing me from Time
Calm the dying flower Calm the growing grass

BEN FRIEDLANDER

In Days of Awe

The stars,

Guided by mathematics,

Shine,

But so slowly, their light

Never arrives

Until

After calculations

Are proven wrong.

And so it is with prayer:

An unwritten vowel

Breathes

Into our fears, and stumbles on,

A consonant without acknowledged meaning.

Fundamental

When we dead

Metaphors awaken,

Those for whom God

Was not first cause

But last word

Will find the literal meaning insufficient.

Let the sea roar,

Its fullness

Also

Clap hands and sing

A new song

To drown this miserable silence.

At the End of the Day

There is no order

In merit:

Henry James, blushing outside

A candle's penumbra,

Can't preserve the clatter

Of typewriter keys

In his brain, but speaks instead

Off the record,

Reversing

The counter-revolution

Of so many inklings

Of pain.

Prophecy

My gluey lips permit

No word to seal

The fate of any crow I ate

For old time's sake.

So turn another unshaved cheek

To face the week

That bears its bosom

To a duller blade: today

Sweetens the coffee-

Colored face of yesterday,

Shutting the stuttering door

On tomorrow.

For an Embedded Journalist

Do you want another spark

Struck off

The old block?

Its head

Spills at the seam

Of a cement bag measuring time

Waiting for nobody

For how long? When people are instruments

Numbered and tagged,

Or done in

By the color of their ink,

Obedience is written in stone.

Blurb

The lyric is a poem

Contained

By hysterical symptoms,

And containing anger

Directed inward.

Expressions of defeat

Disguised as jests,

These poems light

A flaming desert

Bulimics eat for want of sense,

But can't throw up,

And won't digest.

From a Phrase of Simone Weil's
and a Few Stray Thoughts of Hegel

Pull

The liquidity

Of your earnings

Through the eye-

Dropper of a needle, Jesus.

A pencil

Is a stilt

That lets

The sound of my voice

Tower over the silence of your masters.

Hook-nosed martyr,

Here's a shovel

Full of windbag

For your grave.

IOAN FLORA

from Romanian by Adam Sorkin

Radioactive Waste, Guards and Dogs

That autumn, I'm telling you exactly how it happened, a parade of
enormous orange vans showed up,
passed the railroad station like ghosts, headed straight to
the factory and from there, along an access road
that wasn't a road at all,
into the reed thickets of the Danube.
For several nights in a row, men in white coveralls and
men in black coveralls unloaded the vans, removing a sort of can,
a sort of canister, to store them in an officially designated place
inside barbed wire, under a high sky,
with guards and dogs.
And the vans, all of a sudden, it was as if they were swallowed by the earth.
Nobody ever saw them again, nobody could find out anything about them.
In time the dogs disappeared, too, and that left
the one guard, a bored guy with a red bottle-nose
and a joke of a gun, not a real one.
One fine day, the guard took a crowbar and pried open
one of those metal canisters and got a glimpse
of a kind of paint, a wonder, like the crop of a dove
hot for love.

He took it home and painted his tin roof,
which now shone in the sun very like a palace, nothing less.
Then in turn one relative after another showed up, then a neighbor
(and why shouldn't he share it with them?),
to get paint for a gate, a trough, a fence, a rain gutter,
a chicken coop.
The priest came, too, for the steeple, the bells,
the church tower.
Then the guys from Roads and Bridges,
so they could construct the road between the villages A. and C. with
materials from there,

and soon after the school principal and the hospital administrator.
Housewives as well, to prettify their gas stoves,
children, for their bicycles,
coquettes, for their nails or cracked lips.
That's it, the whole place glittered like a carnival!

The most beautiful thing was when the bells tolled evening prayers
at Saint Ilie's.
It was a miracle just to see them, iridescent, gleaming,
as if they were speaking directly in God's ear.
But who could have guessed, my friends, that since then,
in our limbs themselves, there hatched not the serpent but a poison spike,
death in the flesh.

And not only in our bones but also in the potato flower,
in the ground squirrel,
and in the glorious future proclaimed from every podium at every
meeting.

And how happy we were, when we still were!

Targu-Jiu, July 1989

—translated with Elena Borta

On Loneliness, Wells and Graves

"There are wells, why not, that don't have roofs overhead,"
The Lady of Desert Places confesses to the Reporter.
"Even where we ourselves lived, there was a beautiful one of brick,
broad, I couldn't tell you how far down its bottom,
but it must have been quite deep.
It went dry for a time, but I see it's filled with water again.
I don't know where this water came back from,
only that it no longer has any bounds;
when you look into it, you can see it's very deep—
water has somehow risen up in it now."

The Reporter asks whether this forsaken place
(only two residents, plus a few nomadic shepherds following their flocks)
still has a graveyard,
since it no longer has either priest or prayer in the village, its church
a complete ruin.
The Lady of Desert Places (once upon a time a cleaning lady
at the Red Poppy Bakeshop in Timisoara) or, interchangeably, her husband
(a roustabout at the state meat packing plant in the city) replies.
They speak in turn, telling about the three stone crosses,
the rest *have crumbled nearly to nothing*,
about the old times when on the Day of the Virgin Mary—our Little Mary,
people from all over came here to pray
(*maybe once, at most twice, I remember it rained,*
but the rest, sun, bright sun, the finest weather),
about some Germans who showed up with aid and filmed the collapsed
church tower, the nettles.

The epic project *Desert Spaces*.
Viorel Marineasa and Daniel Vighi on foot
(the Day of the Cross, September '97),
traversing the depopulated villages in the Lipova Tableland
around the Gorges of the Mures where the river enters the Banat:
"The project has an artistic dimension, but concomitantly is intended as a
sociological, anthropological and philosophical investigation into loneliness,

alienation and abandonment as phenomena specific to the modern world."

"Let me tell you, nothing causes me more sorrow than the fruit trees,"
The Lady of Desert Places goes on.
"I stand in the weeds and nettles, Jonathan apples drop to the ground below,
and cherries,
pears.
They lie in unmown grass and rot. Nobody does anything about it.

"That's when the deserted land hurts me the worst, when I look at these trees …"

—translated with Alina Carac

Brancusi's House in Hobita

First the *Fireplace Room*, the big hearth with a shelf for plates, a cast-iron kettle,
a clay oil lamp, a lid to put over baking bread,
Cuza's weight from the old days,
a bushel measure, a spoon rack, a salt mill,
the fancy flask for going around to invite neighbors to weddings, wooden spoons,
saltcellar, earthenware bowls,
a round, three-legged table.

To one side, in the *Good Room*, a bed with no mattress,
a horizontal Oltenian frame for hanging clothes,
a loom,
a dowry chest, the wardrobe with a wooden sun inlaid
in the middle of each door.

The *Larder* has no roof now.
This way star dust sprinkles on the eel basket,
the weir, the basket for landing fish,
the wooden saddle, cowbells,
combs for carding wool,
the trap for fox and fitch hung on the wall.

Outside
a large kettle, the barn loft, the cellar with a still for plum brandy,
the upstairs porch,
and especially the spirit of the place, the spirit of wood and stone,
the spherical, circular, elliptical spirit,
the round spirit,
the vertical spirit,
the tetrahedron raking the courtyard grass,
beguiling the stars from the sky.

It's summer, noon, no *Maiastra* or *Muse*,
no *King of Kings* about.
Bugles burnish the air, piercing laments, village fiddlers:
somber and sober, as is only fitting, the cortege snakes by in the street,
the base or maybe the pinnacle of an *Endless Column*.

Copybook

For several moments, edges of text exhale
smell of basement, a garden in rain,
oak leaves, and bark catches the skin of her leg,
not quite slicing through, engraves a chalk mark that
almost burns, dissipates. She can bend to
put her mouth on it, identifies her skin, sweet,
salt, like the yard. She copies pictures of fish
from a library book, traces with colored pencil.
Other lawns interest her. She admires,
follows, drops from the tree. Thirty years later
a Croatian waiter brings hot milk with almond.

The Kiss

after Caravaggio's *The Taking of Christ*

Nothing flickers from the lantern, even though it glows.
Christ leans away, although you say he's leaning forward,
the metalled arm, a fulcrum between pans.

A light, you're right, comes from elsewhere.
They look at him or look away. The crowd's not looking
as he folds into himself, or at the fingers which hover and sting,
sick of gesturing. Only he can feel their breath

and you, so sharp, you know
that only our light reflects off their bodies,
the weight of the glove at his neck.

ZAFER ŞENOCAK

from German by Elizabeth Oehlkers Wright

from Berlin Before the Black Spring

III

sentences that lack nothing ever thought of
except the patience to hear them to the end
to speak like the wind never writes

nothing's left of this square
not even a pair of hackneyed headlines
hardly a lonesome sound
the mystery of a name
it rains only in the cracks it left behind droning
in a pit between two mountains of rubble
a black dot on the map

the day is uncorked
a sip of wine seals the evening
the lonely have a heart-to-heart talk
a scratched record turns on the square
it rains droning and the record paints its tones
all the same to them they say it's raining just what we ordered
the same for all
the lonely stick to their limits

if there were more than one death prowling this city
it would make sense to lay in wait with ten thousand tents
if there were one sound behind its wall
in order to be heard
by one leftover reveler in the square
and by the animals in the garden
that would do

but only the rain is left that paints everything the same
and the producers of headlines
they forget as soon as they've written them
the stand-ins with their poetic inspirations

IV

the fish on the balcony throw their bones to autumn
we staple together all the unclaimed hope in a small room
behind a dark window rusts a bright
window and even from the rust, flowers flash

our prices fall
the gardener trimmed the bushes
weeded the fish bones
walks around the house seven times
dusts the gravestones

on the smooth lawn resembling a desert
our tracks disappear in another's tracks

in despair we move within our own shells
we close the windows with our eyelashes
and listen

V

but what I want to say is
this hunchback buggy is much too quiet
for a breakneck life
and too loud for a secret one

anyone who sees us
between the trunks and flying carpets
ends up blind
the die is cast

be silent now
the road is too steep
all around us fine-tuned ears
too little gravel
bottomless

and your hunchback is too high
the sky too close
the clouds shine through
about to dissolve

it's cast out the window daily
for someone
who thinks of flying
nose too short

he who falters
flies for real

VII

spies step down in public
young men sacrifice their well-groomed baby faces
                              to fast-living action films
one call is enough to elect a new hero

from an empty movie theatre sudden longing for humphrey bogart
ala the west
what a president he would make
the verbs vibrate from phrases they until now have held in check
lead pours into their openings
heavy tongues lifeless snake bodies

from the outline of an endless arm
or sin in aramaic

the hand lets go
breaks

the tongue that still speaks
on large moon craters some place like that
on the coat of a banished god
is subject to change without notice

history the arm invents
won't be wiped away with its sleeve

the drinker makes empty toasts to lost illusions smacking his lips
brother spy embraces brother mass murderer in the back courtyard

IX

the gods love whoever writes to them
and we build temples from their letters
send illegible postcards
from our lives

the doves bury their beaks there
in order to unearth a word
alone on the great square
perhaps a cloud blows a few drops
and shoe heels tumble from empty buildings
that look like giant moving boxes

where are the people
ask the ones writing
in order to be loved
where are the gods
ask the people

XI

the butterfly of the sky and I sit down to eat
and I draw the sun a dark beard
grow older at the long table
with ancient tragedies and empty cup
at this table I drink from the stones
since the dawn of history the table has known only cannibals
and a flesh eating sun
the grottoes burn in the cliffs
beyond it is a beach full of mystery and painted
palm trees
and glass pyramids of skulls

travelers sit at the table without a word
off to see themselves
using their heads to wrestle the ruins in their heads
they scrape the pictures from their eyes
to throw them into a deep well
disappear when a word falls

there is this drunken banker from the seventh floor
who every morning keeps his story to himself
using the same face the same story
every morning in a different language
the way he plunges out the window
whatever he learns as a dead man among the living
he keeps to himself when he steps up to the door

and the woman around forty
who for every lecture at the Urania society
drags a pirate dispatcher into her bedroom
they catch the termites together in the cupboards
and spread them out on the bed
a sawmill

he's still here the boy who's missing
whose corpse in the river I tend to daily
using age-old remedies

when he molds I lose all hope
clear off the table

but as long as the corpse lives
I'll cook up my stories
at this remembered table in the midday heat
table legs in the water
don't let it show
not the fear
not the curiosity
not the longing
as if remembering were female
her legs in the water

XII
throw the books in the water they're burning
throw the books in the water helpless
that's your power not much
grief's more like it
grief and power share nothing

someone comes along
sits down at the shoreline
and starts to write on the water

it's the others
who divide the world up into rooms
they carry the keys on their belts
the waist must grow

the tiger holes up in the wind
I don't want to open the door
I will take nothing from the postman
what will the next message in a bottle bring

don't look around write
when you no longer see land

XIII

out of touch with the events
undermined by my senses
I rush to sell off my intoxication
before the black spring

beneath me traffic comes to a stop in the sewers
file traffickers staple a life's work
the comatose stumble bravely from their holes
out of touch with the events
I sell off my intoxication
before the black spring

I plunder old films
create sound effects
from soundless clips
what the scholars and the street vendors overlooked
stands beside me in the kitchen
next to the steaming tea kettle

at thirty-three I closed my eyes
and disappeared behind my own expression
was it me was it you or was I no one inside me
in dreams I still saddled red horses
and unbound fairy-tale characters from their tracks
while at the gates the man holding the reins bridled
                              his nags into new forms

the images of my own slipping behind the mirror
I open the window it's a faded album
in my hand shards are blooming a springtide of shards
and the blossoms throw smoke-fringed shadows
images long repressed but long from dead
bind themselves to my body like hunchbacks

for example this liquor a friend brought
he smuggled it in from a far-off country in me

the innermost neighborhood
of this liquor whose sharpness is of a knife
whose muddiness is like this region's melancholy
its taste draws me in from the distant past

one swallow tears me away from my wall
another bans me from my country
my melancholy evening
where
among the fishers who rust while working
among the burned throats
of this liquor that allowed me to forget
that it's me
me the city
or you are
am I no one inside me

I know you're all asking me about my life
let's say born around nineteen hundred
at thirty-three I was a torso
that's what they called a boy who's been around
then slipped behind the mirror
I felt around behind me for the smashed pieces
there were the faded albums
and the poets with their patient loyalty
who exhumed me
me
behind my mirror
out of touch with the events

I wish my portrait would have always had cracks
like the ones now ones that last that are for everyone
today in my brightest rags
I wish to be invisible

Registration for Enlightenment

Quiet, please … please, may I have your invention
of the universe in your own likeness. All applicants

anxious to overpraise your proudest accomplishments,
will find advisors available to foster presumption

and self-reverence, stances newly adapted to exhaust
the Transcendent Mind. For aspirants auditing

pretension courses from the Adjunct Professor of
Reluctance, undue credit for exaggerated exegesis

of innermost journeys remains transferable. It is
with the unparalleled solicitude of this institute

that channels are provided which proffer weight
to endangered theses and elective creeds. Never

before have so few meant so little to so many. We
offer an accelerated transition of the irrational

into an improvised dogma that inhibits revelation
through annotated programs of formatted paths.

Bear in mind that Sanctimony may be substituted
for Astral Influence only by remission of the unseen . . .

The Middle Innings

"Let your heart slow down and follow your pitches."
Vern Ruhle, Houston Astros pitching coach

A better tribute would be scraping the trim, wire brushing
the storms, sanding the clapboards down to bare wood
and mixing terps not paint-thinner for the primer, keeping
a spare brush in my back pocket for dusting the sills, the tops

of all the double-hung windows ..., not planting grass. *"What's
the best time to paint?"* from your corny repertoire—*"When
they have the money."* Boom. Sweep the snow off the stairs
and lay on the Battleship Gray or Green Porch & Deck Enamel.

You didn't make all hundred-and-sixty-two games this year,
missing the end of Ripkin's streak and Big Mac's home run
total by twelve. Irresistible to us: statistics and nicknames: The
Splendid Splinter, The Kid, Teddy Ballgame hitting .388 at 39,

Triple Crown winner three times, lifetime batting average .344.
Our cherished pursuit of official accomplishments. You had
the stroke the year the Braves moved from Milwaukee to Atlanta
(*"Lou Burdette—he'd make coffee nervous."*) at an age when

most men rich or not, begin to lean back. The man you made
assistant took your job away, the State of Connecticut your license,
and at fifty-four, you couldn't check your tears as the Sox ripped
single after single off Yankee pitching, Fenway ablaze in adoration.

This lawn's a mess, uneven spots at home, first base, first base line,
and the pitcher's mound; and a worn yellow patch where we dumped
cloudy water after boiling lobsters for someone's birthday. Every
thing's a chance, a time at-bat, but I'm out here morning, noon, and

night, as you'd say, watching, waiting for the first glimpses of grass,
watering this limed and fertilized soil, spraying in long arcs as a
groundskeeper would, wetting the base paths, solicitous
of the blessed infield.   I should be up on a ladder,

with a paint hook and white pants, cutting in sash with one
of your inch-and-a-half China bristle brushes ... but I'm out here
on the new topsoil, amended lawn, under a full moon, watching
the ALCS through a window, with perfect reception of the stars,

taking advantage of the slow second season.

Sixteen Shades of Gray

The angle opens, the horizon
vanishes. Still, for the ten-
thousandth time I work
separations onto a surface.

If there were some resolution,
I could understand, but nothing
shows, nothing moves from head
to heart to hand, but blood.

I stop, and watch intensity
diminish on the glass. Nothing
is detected, the screen oblique,
deflection of an artificial edge.

JACQUELINE WATERS

from Guard of an Eaten Collage: A Guard

(And now you get another picture
of my mind thinking all this,
and know the present terrific moment's
important to me both now
and as snapshot put away
for future soothing nostalgia.
And this gives *you* hope,
though you're no longer yourself,
the quiet white person, loyal only
to the view from your eyes)

Horse

Horse, horse, will you be my mother?
I am a horse. I cannot be your mother.

Think
Of the point at which a disturbance
Intersects itself
To show which side it supports: nobleness
Or misfitness: think of a tampered-with
Racehorse assigned
To the usual oval now think
Of a heat-seeking
Ejaculation into
A can of no-name
Asparagus tips

Stop giving me that job

Think of the weather, fallen from
High, no longer able t-
o develop, how it can
Only sustain those
Left to its
Consequence: can only excite those left
To care

Would you like to hear a poem I found it in the *Post* it's called The Response

"The Response"

Air-defense planes
were scrambled
but pilots did not
know where to go
or what targets
they were
to interrupt

Once a shootdown
order was given it
was not communicated
to the pilots

Stop giving me that job

Ascend, sad thoughts, on golden wings
And implore heaven to freeze up its seams
That no bad martyr will ever get in
To strum the harp
Or make prophetic utterance

　　　*

Take your seats and clam up
Ask yourself this as you

Clam: have you
Ever done more than faint
Cry some tears
Holding your face in your hands
With one eye open
Peering between two fingers
To see if anyone sees?
Sees *you*? I haven't known
What will happen
Very long. We have a will, we find it
Thwarted, this creates
Irritation, the origin of which,
Over time, grows mysterious.
Such mystery provokes
Our intelligence, which then provides
Answers, answers *born* (don't forget) of irritation, and we'll pretend,
And say stuff, and try to make friends, but in our heads this
Leftover feeling after profound
Thwartedness

Behold, I am against you

Hey handguns, assault rifles, marijuana and
crack
        with broccoli to chew
I have to kill $1 of time
        Was there in the room
some lie I said
that has come true?

Every time I put my head to sleep
Consciousness, aiming to interpret
The guilty twinge, intercepts either
The consciousness of Conscience or the Residue
Of recollected Taunts, buzzed in twice, through the same
Poorly locked door
Would you like to hear a poem it's called Protecto

"Protecto"

Subjects pick out the light
and proceed to get
habituated to it

People focused on their hands
get better pry times
with the pry-point
of the hammer claw

                    *

I like you
When I think of you
But I don't return to you—I don't, that is, *oblige*
To learn if only by experiencing
Dissatisfaction with all that came before
That things illuminate a nice
October evening: here have a little more of it

They themselves become what they behold

You don't see
Them, I see
Them, they are
Hunting me
Down yet I
Must stay on

This is <u>serious</u> this is <u>hoaxes</u> we're not just
Fucking around I mean wake the
Fuck up you filthy ride hogs

Dear man and/or lady, I have tried to guard your poem but now
you and I exchange looks the way normal people exchange money:
man and lady, you and I can't both be guards. If I tell you this in

such words as will make you think, make you live up to your
thinking, have I not done well in telling? Early in my career I
guarded a pharmacy, a real masterpiece of variety, and it was out
of this pilgrim-motive that I developed a formula for manufacturing
guards but then
Like a fool
Started individualizing
Each one

Listen to this thing from the Apocrypha:

"The days will come when vines will grow every one of which will
have ten thousand branches, and on each branch there will be
ten thousand twigs and on each twig ten thousand shoots and on
each shoot ten thousand clusters will grow and on each cluster ten
thousand grapes, and every single grape, when pressed, will yield five
and twenty barrels of wine. And when any one of the saints lays hold
of a cluster, another cluster shall cry out: I am better, take me."

                *

When I'm up in the club
I think about
Shrinking down and running the length of a dart
Shot to the floor of the club

Handsome blue horse, soft yellow duck
I think about the dumbest thing is to sing
To train a little monkey
To be a little man
With a stamp of the foot
And a shake of the head

JACK COLLOM   LYN HEJINIAN

*In 1992, having met at the Naropa Summer Writing Program, Jack Col-
lom and Lyn Hejinian began composing poems collaboratively. They opted
to communicate through the mail rather than utilize a faster technology,
in part because Jack was not (and is not) a computer user, but also so as
to preserve the unhurried pace of the more traditional, contemplative
epistolary space.*

*Beginning with the exchange of free-verse lines that (some 300 mail-
ings later) became* Sunflower *(originally published by The Figures in
2000), they gradually multiplied and diversified their projects. Soon, a
typical exchange would include ten or so formally different works.*

*Generous excerpts from one of these longterm exchanges, "Interview," is
what appears in this volume of Zoland Poetry. Over the years they have
developed a repertoire of forms and procedures, all intended to extend
the possibilities for invention, play, and the unfolding of unforeseeable
meaning. Both poets embrace collaborative authorship as a means of chal-
lenging aesthetic preconceptions, including their own. In the process, they
frequently venture across thematic limits, as well, discovering unexpected
coherences. The poems often give themselves over to pleasure, but they are
governed by the logic of poetic language and they carry considerable meta-
physical depth.*

Lyn Hejinian: "I"? I suppose I'm the result of numerous contingen-
cies, most of which I didn't warrant or notice, and the source of
a few others, most of which I can't promise or predict. "We," says
Thoreau—"we" and "ourselves"—but for the moment, asserting my
singularity, I'll say "I" and "myself": "I find myself in a world that is
already planted, but is also still being planted, as at first." There is no
evidence of progress in the seasonal model. Natural science has to be
content with knowledge. And poetry, too?

Jack Collom: Well, it depends (like water in a well) on words being
repeated twice, which oddly enough gives them an even chance of
"survival through substance," since three dimensions are better than
one and matter at least lives in memory. Form just lives, but poetry
has, meanwhile, gone out, I find. Which indicates it's well. Are you
familiar with some of its haunts?

LH: Language isn't ghostly, really. And, with the sun behind me, the shadow of my head on the table bears no relation to the word "head." So poetry, as I see it, has no haunts. But what if, instead, we propose that poetry itself is a haunt—whose would it be, or what's? No; I'll phrase the question differently: Is your waking life very different from the life you dream when asleep?

JC: When I'm awake I dream of the places that the great blue heron frequents; when I'm asleep I think of the heron itself. In the morning I imagine a ghost and the word "ghost" having an argument: "Is!" "Isn't!" "Is!" "Isn't!" "Is!" "Isn't!" until the heron, whose head casts no shadow, surprises them by coming to a point. Frogs Beware! What's wrong with this picture?

LH: Nothing that isn't wrong with any picture: its stability and the lack of shadow. What I value most about birds (and seek to emulate as best I can) is that they no sooner come to a point than they leave it again. Where they land is never more important than their flying. They are musical in this—more musical in this than in their singing. And because they seek the air, they are always casting changing shadows. I'm reminded of a story (I've told it before) that was told to me by Mohammed Salikh, an Uzbek poet (and hereditary prince). He called it a ghost story and claimed to have dreamed it. He was flying over the desert in search of his mother. He spotted her and tried to land but couldn't because he had no shadow. Then his mother threw her cloak onto the ground to make a shadow for him and he landed. It's our shadow that attaches us to life, he said. Shadow, experience, action, living—writing is about these, not about literature.

[....]

LH: Does your belief system include rain?

JC: My belief system *is* rain. When it comes (gains emphasis), things grow, but if it dominates for too long everything floods and the living creatures (plants too) drown. Light's skepticism clarifies but simply doesn't provide the "glue" that might make context palpable. Left to themselves, these two qualities (rain and light) tend to go wild. The researcher returns from his or her coffee break and finds dichotomy has become a pincushion of aching flesh. Are you married?

LH: Repeatedly, day by day, and willfully, with artichoke in pot rather than pin in cushion. Conviviality is a splendid context for crossing from Mondays to Tuesdays and beyond. What are your favorite foods? And do they figure in your poetry? And if so, what function do they serve?

JC: I've said for years my favorite food is bacon in order to create the impression of a wild, risky, red-streaked man, but now my favorite food is anything other folks drop on the floor. It goes without saying that these favoritisms, these "roving forks of light," figure in my poetry. Their function is to make a hash of experience. How has your writing changed since you were a tiny child?

LH: I wrote entirely in crayon, avoiding "flesh," until I was nineteen. From 19 to 24 I wrote autobiographies, though they were never my own. From 24 to 27 I used nouns as verbs and verbs as nouns. In 1968 I began to write on a portable Olivetti and hoped to become as Italian as Audrey Hepburn. Thirty years later I wrote "Yesterday is gone and never was / And here it is / So we can go to bed with unity of purpose / And crave more of the temperament of life in life's philosophy." I have increased my confusion. Did you ever work as a cowboy? Do you like horses? If you had a horse, what would you call him?

JC: I worked as a cowboy but the job at hand was poet. I say "*as* a cowboy" because I like the rhythm (*as* a cowboy, *as* a cowboy) but, too, because in my compositions I twirl a loop at anything that moves. Nevertheless, I have no skills. I like horses in about the way an arctic fox likes the United States. If I had one (horse) I'd call her Mare Nostrum. What is humor, and what is humor to you?

LH: I couldn't answer that right off the bat and looked the word up, and *there's* a humorous notion, that of looking a word *up*, or it would be if one were of a lecherous cast of mind and *there's* another, that of casting a mind, like a fly on a line at the end of a pole or the discus (which I almost wrote as "discuss") thrown by the idealized athlete or the mold for a statue of a general on his horse or admiral on his rock or pensive poet—Rilke, say, or Pushkin. I've seen many statues of Pushkin and none of Rilke. Humor is a temporary state of mind imposed by circumstances. It's an unpredictable and unreasoning inclination. It's a whim, in fact. It's the capacity to discover something ludicrous or incongruous and that brings me to my next question: Do you think that, as so many of the best young poets are shifting from verse forms to prose (or, to use Clark Coolidge's term, prosoid) forms, they are doing so so as to write autobiographies?

JC: They are. Let's just get that down plain and then go on: having begun the *autobiographical*, obviously, spread, into (oh shit) VITA-MINS spelled backwards or some such, SO: a bubble of conceptual inebriation leads into vision of white giant house in back fields, six-ties, murmurs at the stove, pure bird classification, orange ... how do you chop single words out of history?

LH: Metaphorically, of course, but angrily, too. You can *stir* the word *short*, of course; you can *try this*—you can call the U.S. President a tot whose favorite *toy is his shit rot*. Probably you should and many do and so it goes. But, returning to history, one cannot see clearly what has been lost. Of course, if feelings of shame result, one can say that what's been lost is self-esteem. And if one is weeping, perhaps loved ones have died. But can one return to history after "single words" have been chopped out of it?

JC: To not return to history is to die, and become history. Which raises various specters, such as one's tininess in the immensity, for one, and living defined as dancing feet for another. Maybe if we combine the two visions we can see consciousness as a flea, wonder as an itch, and life as a scratch. Do you find that "single" words burgeon like (word) in a petri dish?

LH: Just as algae make sense and roses are roses? Yes. Words seem destined to oscillate perpetually among the various forms of sen-tence. It has been said that there is an inevitable conflict between the aspirations of men (sic) of letters and the chatty public—but the public when in public (which is the only time the public *is* the public) says hardly anything at all. Think of the people shopping in a mall. Are you thinking of people shopping in a mall?

JC: No, I'm thinking of you saying, "Are you thinking of people shopping in a mall?" But a mall is a sea of variegated speech—no room for the stroller to insert a word even if she (sic) has the breath for it. When they are sitting or standing ingesting something the public becomes a sea of variegated speech itself—actual speech, which is almost indistinguishable from a landfill, not to mention the gulls thronging and squawking upon it. Are you thinking of the gulls thronging and squawking upon it? No, my real question is, How do you feel at parties?

LH: Frantic, eager and apart: "Hysterically convivial and engaged, smiling while talking to myself, I stood alone at the top of the stairs while the brilliant flushed philosopher waved a baby blanket in the air as if signalling—battle? surrender?"—that's a typical festive moment (from my perspective). "Two months later the child, a boy, was born and they called him Leon but his name was George, which disappointed his mother's parents and goes to show that there are many kinds as well as degrees of distance (as of disturbance)." The party goes on just as a story does, and sometimes one gains the greatest pleasure by squeezing one's thoughts into the interstices.

[....]

LH: What's the first thing—no cheating here—what's the *very first* thing that occurs to you when you come upon a silent butler?

JC: Marcel Marceau peering haughtily down Roman cartilage. Just kidding—but I *didn't* cheat—and the reason to kid is that I can't quite think what a silent butler is, or rather can't think what a silent butler quite is. A machine that—opens the door? Serves drinks? So I guess the very first thing that *would* occur to me would be a germ of speculation about how the abundance of hybrids currently confuses human thought, that is, how it kicks candy-coated ball bearings into the typical mental stream. Do you like abnormal subdividings?

LH: As in cancer cells? No way! Anyway, hybridity results from conjunction—and I like conjunctions, yes I do! Although meanwhile but then however, etc.—forever. There's a lot of future in any given conjunction, none in a subdivision. Think of the desert—a deserted desert—no one around, not even you or me, unimaginable—hot, the dirt pale, acrid, a mix of dessicated things—got any notion where that thought was going? Ever had the sense that you were reading someone's mind?

JC: No, I have no notion where that thought was going, except it was about to turn the corner into beauty. And that would've shown subdividings as being intimate conjunctions—lit up the old intentional fallacy. As for reading minds, not much beyond the usual perceptions of unworthy motives. I mean (by "usual") that "everybody" "these days" is uncritically involved in this postFreudian interpersonal fascism which consists of invalidating anything anybody says by thinking how that thing-said might be at least tinged with falsity and then assuming the worst. I try to avoid this type of thinking because of my goodness. Do you think men are sweet because they're limited by logic?

LH: I don't think "men," taken categorically, either as the male of the human species or as the human species ("mankind") generally, *are* sweet, nor do I think that, for the best of you/us, logic is limiting. But you are trying to get at something here—something about the pathos of our (whoever "we" are) attempts to think well, and the melancholy (or even despair) that pervades our awareness of the history of our having not done so. We are failures, and we continue to be so on a daily basis. The self-critical and interpersonal criticism that would help us get things better produces anxiety. Is that process—the process of the contentious community—what you mean by "postFreudian interpersonal fascism"? No—that can't be it. What do you mean?

JC: I mean, I mean, it's a question of authority. In order to properly undercut the authority of a statement (anyone's any-statement—as if we could say what-is), many people educated to recognize the subconscious mind have made a virtual statement of the anti-statement critique. That is, the wisdom of interpretive process has been arrogated willy-nilly and in whole chunks by any (inadvertent) listener. This has become routine, and routinization of anything, even rebellion, amounts to unjust authority. After years of study, someone says, "Much of Earth's soil is washing away many times faster than replacement soil can be formed," and someone else cries, "This elitist treehugger wants to deprive good Americans of their livelihoods just so he/she can wallow in a private park!" However, interpretation should depend on a sense of its own relativity as much as on the world's. But someone will say to this paragraph, "You just want to rationalize a social order you're comfortable with." What's your take on confusion?

LH: Confusion is the better part of dialectics. There are countless situations about which each single position, however carefully considered and however in some respects laudable, is properly assailable and ultimately untenable. The really courageous thinkers are those who take up a position and then shovel the sand out from under themselves (or, as they say, deconstruct it) and then take up an alternative position only to do the same, the point being that WE are the site of the confusion. We're the co-creators of the problem. We shouldn't even grow narcissistically self-congratulatory about our embrace of confusion. Do you wake in the middle of the night filled with terror?

JC: No, I don't wake in the middle of the night filled with terror. But I do think that even the finest conversations, unless they are playful, are like the proverbial "ships passing in the night." That is, that's their geometry. The different speech-balloons are only tangentially, temporarily, and partially connected, by a certain liquid expanse. They don't answer to each other; each cherishes its sovereign cluster of lights. Yet they may send across their captains to share a drink and swap lore. To me, the risk with deconstruction is that it places a torpedo in the hands of an alleycat. Too much democracy! Democracy's virtue is its inefficiency. Do you wake in the middle of the night filled with terror?

LH: Yes. Terror that the ships will collide and terror that they will pass just beyond sight of each other. One wants both/neither to be known—exposed in one's cabin eating crackers and butter—and/nor to be a secret. One wants to keep possession of one's secrets but not to be one—or is it the other way around: One wants to surrender one's secrets to a "true friend" but to remain one, even (or especially) to oneself. It is true that though mirrors don't lie, we nonetheless lie to mirrors; old women know this to be true, but I ask myself, do old men? Many writers have spoken, in one way or another, of their love of "easeful death." They mean their own, not that of their child or friend. I am afraid of death, but not of my own.

[....]

LH: Do you have any idea what "C.P.T." refers to in the last stanza of Langston Hughes's poem "Dancer" (from *Montage of a Dream*

Deferred)—"Even a great dancer / can't C.P.T./ a show"?

JC: Conjure-Pirate-Treasure   Colette-Proust-Tanguy
Conceive-Preach-Time   Cougar-Panther-Tiger
Completely-Pump-Thump   Compensate-Previous-Thud
Cool-Prime-Tandaradei!   Carve-Preen-TrickleCorn-Peach-Tomato
Click-Prick-Trick   Connect-Perfection-To Cock-Poodle-Too

No, I don't. Sorry. What will American poetry be like in 100 years?

LH: Something American, though what "American" will mean in 100 years is hard to know. America is an imaginary site. The native peoples didn't conceive of it as a geo-political entity and the Europeans who did so were dreaming. Lasciviously, in some cases—as in John Donne's wonderful/awful "Elegie: Going to Bed":

> Your gown going off, such beautious state reveals,
> As when from flowry meads th'hills shadowe steales.
> Off with that wyerie Coronet and shew
> The haiery Diadem which on you doth grow:
> ....
> Licence my roaving hands, and let them go,
> Behind, before, above, between, below.
> O my America! my new-found-land,
> My kingdome, safeliest when with one man man'd,
> My Myne of precious stones: My Emperie,
> How blest am I in this discovering thee!

But there was something I wanted to ask you … Fuck! What were we talking about just before the phone rang?

JC: I think it was golden-ratio reasoning, in which each assertion is 1.618 times bolder than the one before. The precision of it all typically knocks the socks off the interlocutor, who crawls into bed shivering from the top down and begins reading *In the Belly of the Beast* with a flashlight till his/her parents, awakened by the sound of pages turning like the lapping of waves on some Madagascar shore, where two lemurs are gathering coco shells, row into the room and make their macro-micro demands. How do you quiet down a horse after it's been spooked by avalanche or hungry puma?

LH: You ride it again past the site of the fright to show that the danger has moved away. This can take a lot of time—it's like remastering a tape in an old studio with quirky equipment near an airport.

[....]

JC: Did you ever wonder thus: "Why am I (who must be the universal subjective) me?"

LH: Not in precisely those terms. But the question, "Why am I *this* rather than *that*?" was a question that recurred throughout my childhood and youth, and thinking about it may have provided me with the grounds for empathy later on. The matter of being this particular person was, to me, always framework for considering the arbitrariness (and, often, the cruelty) of circumstances. That is, when I looked at my enviable (so they seemed to me and so they were) circumstances, I was amazed that I hadn't been born into some other harsher set, along with the people that I tended to think about (victims of history's many atrocities), even almost to identify with. Later, in adulthood (even to this day), I have often succumbed to the temptation to wonder how it is that I am not a duck, or jellyfish, or tiger in the wild. Or a cowboy or doctor (both things I once wanted to "be"). If you had another life to live, what would you be?

JC: I don't know. I wanted to be a red fox when I was small. Do you mean reincarnation when you say "another life to live"? If so, I'd like to be, oh, a parrot in the wilds of the Amazon. And, if there's one there may be more: a quicker Jack. Now you may ask yourself a question. What will it be?

LH: I'd like to ask my parents how they reacted to the rounding up and incarceration of California's Japanese-Americans in March of 1942. Were they outraged? Going by what I witnessed later of their reactions to racist paranoia and bigotry, they would have been. But California politicians and the San Francisco newspapers had been waging a virulent anti-Japanese campaign for decades—might they have been somewhat persuaded by it? They were living in San Francisco; my father had joined Naval Intelligence and was awaiting orders; I was 10 months old. About ten years later, when he refused to join a protest against the Greek grocery store owner's purchasing a house on our street, my father was verbally attacked on our front porch by a Berkeley "neighborhood preservations committee" for being a "pinko" and a "nigger-lover." When I once asked my mother about wartime San Francisco, she described a somewhat rough transition into complex modernity of a culture that sounded like something transplanted from New England by a mercantile class that liked proximity to the Pacific and the artifactual culture of Asia. She described cultural "shocks" occasioned by the war but said nothing of the city's Japanese and concentration camps. Do you know the current theory explaining the toppling of the enormous statues on Easter Island?

JC: No. I read about it (if it's still "the current" theory) recently, but memory failed me again, as it does more and more frequently. It's as if I fail to pay enough attention to the factors that feed memory, such as nutrition, good study habits, temperance, the cultivation of an elastic sense of time … what else? It's as if I were chopping down the forest, as it were, of my mental ecosystem in my greed for ceremonial fires and daily luxurious warmth. Following which, of course, my contextual landscape erodes away and the layeredness on which life depends succumbs to the "gravity of the situation." Oh, levitation might create a memory manqué.… I take solace in the fact that even a fallen memory leaves a kind of geometry in the air.

[….]

LH: Is there a single poet with whom you would most want to argue?

JC: Yeah, and it's happening in the most amiable way. Aside from you, I would pick the poet, or two, I love the most: Hopkins and (of late years) Gertrude Stein. That there's *so* much to argue with in each case probably reveals that I make things difficult for myself. But should one make things easy for oneself? What would one be easing the way for? Hopkins, if he sat across the table from me, might inquire, while twirling and measuring a butternut leaf, why I diffuse myself like a minor oil spill. I'd be thrilled. I would ask Stein (if I could crawl into her portrait) why she is so modest. What is (are) your favorite number(s)?

LH: 3 (for dialectics), 7 (for its harping on and then undermining dialects), and 9 (for good luck, rhythm, and rhyme). Under duress—

that is to say, when in a real panic, I recite numbers in random sets to myself. The set is limited to numbers under 100: e.g., ten, two, forty, ninety-two, three, etc. Repetitions are permissible, so the sequence is potentially infinite. I'm not allowed to "go back" on a number. It's the equivalent of "automatic writing": the automatic numbering of distress, ever in quest of pattern and, from pattern, information. Do you use all ten fingers when you type or do you, raptor-like, "hunt and peck"?

JC: I hunt and peck, though after fifty-plus years the hunt's become a twitch. I typed while in the Air Force; after I'd got up to sixty words a minute with my forefingers I was sent to a two-week typing school and taught to type sixty-per with ten fingers. But then I reverted immediately to hunt-&-peck because I fancied its idiosyncrasy. Incidentally, Ron Padgett hunts and pecks with a great number of his fingers. Of late, I've been slowed: my left hand's poor at fine movement, from nerve damage, and I hold my left forefinger firmly against thumb and middle finger to strike the keys. Also, my right forefinger has become useless through an infection (tendon damage?) and I've substituted the middle finger. I'm not sure about the effect of all this middle-finger employment on my poetic style. Poor eyesight and the scattering of mental control also play their parts. At any rate it's, if we choose a bird simile, more vulturine than raptorlike, though I prefer a fresh kill. I do love typing inordinately.

LH: What book(s) are you currently reading?

JC: Looking through my chief workroom/bedroom stacks, I find *Natural History* magazine, Alice Notley's Naropa Summer Writing Program handout, "Bed" (Summer Writing Program magazine), *Shirley Shirley* by Alicia Askenase, *High Country News*, *Sound Nets* by Richard Martin, *I Was Going to Use That* by Rob Geisen, a Michael Moore generic email, poems by Carmen Vigil, *Teachers & Writers* summer issue, *The Invisible City* (ed. Marcella Durand), *The Distressed Look* and *God Never Dies* by Joanne Kyger, *New Goose* by Lorine Niedecker, a Rachel Levitsky ms., *I My Feet* by Gerhard Rühm, *Infinity Subsections* by Mark DuCharme, *An Evolution of Writing Ideas, and Vice Versa,* by me, "Geochemical Evidence for Oxygenated Bottom Waters During Deposition of Fossiliferous Strata of the Burgess Shale Formation" by Christopher Collom, *My Life in the Nineties* by you, *Harper's* magazine (2), *Bombay Gin 30*, *Austerlitz* by W. G. Sebald, *The Paris Stories* by Laird Hunt, *The Seasons* and *Rivers & Birds* by Merrill Gilfillan, *Guns, Germs, and Steel* by Jared Diamond, *Music of the Spheres* by Guy Murchie (many untouched for somewhile). And these represent just the fin of the shark (don't count new Fish Drum stuff). I'm a mess. I think I have cataracts. Who's winning, in your book, the city or the country?

LH: I remember that some years ago I said to you or wrote to you or thought to say or write to you—I remember wanting you to see (and acknowledge) that environmentalist concerns might be contrary to the interests of ordinary people. In the process of closing down corporate exploitation, real and good people suffer, and not in some abstract sense but really, truly, in the very heart of their lives. I wanted you to see that—and of course now, these years of friendship later, I know that you've seen that. It's a complicated opposition, and probably not a valid one, that of country vs. city. What is either, that it might win? And what might it win? Countrification (sounds like something the British upper-classes did, or that movie star Americans do when buying land in New Mexico)? Citification? In my own heart, the country (you do mean rurality, right, and not the USA as a patriot's heaven?) wins—that is to say, in a battle (but there is none) for my devotion. And yet, at the same time, I have had (and have) a good life in the semi-city of Berkeley, California. To live here is not to lose.

> [....]

JC: How close do you like to be to things?

LH: Generally, I like to be close enough to things to see them and know what they are, but there are exceptions to that. I like to keep a good distance between myself and things that stink or threaten. And I like to get very close to things that provoke my curiosity (even, as in the case of the golden orb spiders now abundant in the backyards of Berkeley, when they threaten—which occasionally the spiders do, rearing up, wagging their front legs, and shaking the web) so as to see their obscurer elements or study their particular features. Recently, I have felt myself getting closer and closer to understanding certain complex poems—Zukofsky's "A," for example. Or to put it another way, I find that I have come to a point in time (my time or the world's, I'm not sure which) where I can participate in such poems with feelings that I call "understanding"—exhilarated, in effect. What work of literature that you didn't write do you wish you had?

JC: I often wish, as I read, poetry especially, that I had written or, even more, could write what I'm reading, but I try to shake such feelings as being flare-ups of ego-sickness and not a receptive way to read. (Pause.) Picking from literally thousands of possibles, I'll mention Anne Carson's piece in *The Best American Poetry 2004*, "Gnosticism." What I envy, miss, is her familiarity with the landscape so that she can, having passed through abstract coherence (of Gnosticism) and through concrete versions of and off it, pass into a glorious, sour chaos, nursing its logic. Work energy, non-dilettante.

[....]

JC: Do you ever become angry with me?

LH: No. Back when we first started writing works together, I got frustrated sometimes when you took what I took to be a "silly" turn where I wanted a "serious" continuation of something, but I got over that pretty fast. It was just that I couldn't keep up with your imaginative pace. Comedy is serious and the so-called "silly turn" can advance thought at high velocities that "seriousness" can't achieve. The first result of our beginning to write together was our book *Sunflower*; my book *A Border Comedy*—my favorite of all my writings—became the continuation of the truly full "something" you introduced me to. Are you ever angry at me?

JC: No. I've felt fretful at what I've taken to be, or to include, mere serenity. But that's just where I've learned the deepest, dearest lessons, which involve linguistic patience, the forming of a partnership with, rather than a use (abuse) of time, and even the ways work's exercise are endless—but then indeed snap off properly at personality's foot. (Our colloquies sail on silvery tracks; I'm sure *if* we were tossed together for a time we'd find extravagances of objectionability....) Who are your favorite novelists?

LH: That's easy: Marcel Proust and Charles Dickens and Henry

James are my favorite novelists. I enormously admire Melville, too, but his imagination is always utterly unfamiliar to me, so I haven't the warm affection and sense of affinity with Melville's work that "favorite" implies (to me, at least). But, having said that, why do I feel that "favor" requires some kind of "coziness"? Surely it must be because I imagine the social or psychic space in which reading novels occurs to be some kind of happy, untrammeled site. But why should reading novels be assumed to be an intimate activity? I don't think of reading poetry in those terms. If there is a movie/film that particularly terrified you, what is it?

JC: I think of *The Uninvited*, with Gail Russell and Ray Milland. The thing was, I saw it as a child, when a movie could terrify me (I've been told, lately, it's a mediocre movie, but I remember, or remember remembering, a sudden door slam that was stunning ((or perhaps wakening))). By now, movie fears have become merely delicious (and maybe that was part of it then). By now, I'm afraid that somebody in a given movie is going to deceive someone else, or be misunderstood (almost the same), and I get so uncomfortable it's almost like terror. Then it's difficult to crawl out of one "parenthesis" and into the next.

[....]

JC: What's your earliest memory?

LH: "A moment yellow." That's the opening phrase of my book *My Life* and as far as I know the opening phrase of my conscious life. If it is a memory at all and not some strange brain-buzzed shimmer that stands in for memory, then it records my coming upon a dandelion or buttercup on a tiny patch of grass behind the house on Filbert Street in San Francisco that my paternal grandfather had bought for my parents. I must have been lying on my stomach, legs kicking, head up, nose to nose with the flower. My father may have been in uniform. Or perhaps he wasn't—is it possible that this memory is (as I feel it is) so early that I'm not yet 7 months old (as I was when the Japanese bombed Pearl Harbor)? In any case, the memory is *vivid* with *particular* color—nothing like the night (of murky absolutism) "when all cows look black." Will you tell me about your own military service?

JC: USAF 4 years. Polished shoes and blanket tight, AF 16 422 508 reporting for duty SIR. Enlisted in Chicago (to avoid Korean War draft), Basic Training outside San Francisco, where I got my now 52-year-old tattoo. Loved marching, became squad leader. Then they made me a Remington Ranger (clerk-typist). Stateside Greenville, South Carolina, where I was jailed overnight for staggering drunkenly down the sidewalk, lost a stripe; Altus, Oklahoma; ASAP overseas. Tripoli, Libya. Typed Morning Reports all day with 2 fingers, read *Moby Dick* in a Quonset hut. Wandered endlessly, on pass, among white buildings, Hadrian's Arch, stopping for beers in Italian bars (falling through the roof of one, where I'd clambered, from reading *Faust*, to watch the foot traffic on Sharia Istaklal). TDY in Athens & Rome, Troop-Carrier Wing Detachments. Reassigned Neubiberg, near Munich, where, in the Havana Bar, I met a hefty Bavarian woman who laughed when I pulled a peanut butter sandwich from my pocket. Whom I later married. 4 years up, released from AD, NYC (cold magnet where I lived, surveyed, attended operas, before returning to Munich).

[....]

LH: Have you ever felt that some path in life you wanted to follow was closed to you—and if so, why (what closed it off)?

JC: Scholarship. Or being scholarly. It's partly a path, partly a floodplain. I graduated from an unaccredited high school (tiny mountain town) and was told I was only eligible to attend the state agricultural school. Also, my parents had no money (but they bravely, frugally sent me to A & M). Backwaters education has a simpler structure, more like checkers thinking than the (urban) emotional complex of chess. One sees logic more starkly. During four Air Force years I read a lot, but my reading was shaped like a barracks. Then I married and worked; amid that schedule I could write or study, not both. And I've inherited and moistened a memory scattered and Alzheimeresque. Well, boo hoo, but I think a level of laziness was/is more crucial in my failure to become a scholar (just a level or 2, like a layer of water in a stack of plywood). Also excess of eagerness (funny word "eager"; vinegar is eager wine; eager is a point, gives birth to a line, not a web; yet a number of points makes a field, which is eventual ground …). (Philip Whalen became a scholar against great odds—perhaps some scholar should split and classify the types of stubbornness.) What can you say about your moment-to-moment writing process(es)?

LH: For years my processes have been just that, "moment-to-moment," such that all the events that are generated aesthetically and/or philosophically have occurred at the surprising moments where one thing unexpectedly meets another and, as it were, forges a relationship with it. This has been the nature of my process for years—working within microcosmic points of encounter, with very little idea (and very little desire to have an idea) of what's about to happen (or, sometimes, of what it is that *has* happened). But suddenly that kind of engagement doesn't seem to be working as well as it did for so long, and I find myself having to step back, hold things in mind, sustain some kind of "over view." I don't want to suggest that I am seeking to seize control of the writing; it's just that I can't manage to proceed (at least with my current projects) completely in the dark—though staying in the dark remains as relevant thematically now as it was procedurally before. What's your favorite color?

JC: Sunday-go-to-meeting: orange (Saturday too). Weekdays brown. I used to love chocolate brown but now favor a range of browns, including "dull" ones. In fact, I like odd combinations above all. My favorite color is—not plaid but something holding a knothole to a Matisse might reveal. Is that too precious? Well, slosh some Elmer's glue and sprinkle fine dust on it. Red! When I was a kid, *blue* was my fave. Lifted me up (he says greenly). Never used to like red. Seemed aggressive. Now I see red's tremble under the extroversion. Bison. Chartreuse. How do you get along with numbers?

LH: Uncomfortably, I suppose, although now and then, without calculating, I may "know" the sum of two numbers the way I "know" the name of some flower ("Henderson's shooting star!" "coreopsis!"). But mostly, though I trust that the name I come up with for a flower is the name it's known by among humans locally, I virtually never, when it comes to numbers, trust that the sum I sense is the right one. Then again, more than sometimes, structurally I use number to organize and shape material. *My Life*, for example, consists of 47 sections/poems each 47 sentences long. I was 47 years old when I wrote it. Now I'm 63, and that number has little bearing on my sense of myself—in my movie of myself, I'm older than that and much younger. Was "the Donald Allen anthology" (*The New American Poetry: 1945–1960*) important for you?

JC: It was as important for me as marriage. I was living in the Polish-Russian factory town of Seymour, Connecticut, with Traudl, working in the brassmill, writing poetry inspired by what I could find in Louis Untermeyer anthologies, when Stan Brakhage sent it to me in 1960 or '61. At first I was shocked by its roughness and what I took to be the carelessness of writing "immediately." I was very soon a convert. In fact, I'd been looking desperately for ways out of convention's deathgrip (not to say the convert doesn't drag all baggage into new room; not to say new room wasn't envisioned; but permissions can be as simple as "Oh, you can write what's in front of you?" "All day long?"). Early enthusiasms were Olson (especially the essay), Dorn, Wieners, Ashbery. Others too, or soon. I took the revolution to be deep-down, that is, aesthetic. It was all a language-allure. Many people are stuck with just one revolution, but I think the opposite is true too: that revolution foments revolution, sometimes dragging it kicking and screaming from reluctant context, as the inclusion of women. Was (is) the Allen anthology important for you?

LH: Absolutely, and I wish I could remember as clearly as you do how it came to me, and when. The binding of my original Grove Press edition fell apart long ago, but I still have the "volume," in its disrepair, held together with a length of string tied in a bow. Releasing the pages, I find no clue as to when or where I was when I read it, but I am almost positive that it would have been Cambridge (Massachusetts) in 1961 or 1962, when I was still in college. I'd read (and imitated) a lot of e. e. cummings's poems with enthusiasm and a sense of discovery in high school; I'd read *Ulysses* with a sense of being in on a secret and I'd read *Mrs. Dalloway* with a sense of familiarity. In early 1960 I had come across a copy of Ferlinghetti's *Coney Island of the Mind* and Kenneth Patchen's *Journal of Albion Moonlight* (along with various slender volumes of his poems), and in May 1962 on my 21st birthday Ken Irby gave me a copy of Creeley's *For Love*. The Donald Allen anthology must have come my way around then: 1961, 1962. Like you, I was drawn to Olson; I loved Brother Antoninus's "A Canticle to the Waterbirds," the McClure poems, the O'Hara poems, the Creeley poems. I thought John Berryman's *Dream Songs* (not, of course, in the anthology) were amazing, and I was just beginning to read Wallace Stevens. It all adds up, I suppose, and can't be reduced down. I didn't notice that there were so few women, I didn't consider the social politics that such a volume represented at all. The poetry was the thing, and I could (so it seemed) identify with anyone writing it. How do you start a poem?

JC: I used to just sit and start. Lately (for years) much of my actual wordage has come via collaborations, so the start is a bargain, relatively responsibility-free. But *most* of the collaborations serve, it turns out, as keeping a hand in, and as conversation. I do learn from them, over and over (and the repetition's necessary), about multiple causes, multiple input, degrees of out-of-control, uses of spontaneity. The past year especially I've been "collaborating with myself": starting a series of poems but writing only one line into each, until a day has passed and it's time for another line each. Thus I get a more horizontal feel within process. The "rules" with which I begin such a series are meant to be balanced between extremes of openness and closedness—extremes to emphasize the physical, to discourage "humanistic" cogitation. The open/closed approach is developed from my criteria for classroom work with children. Another aspect of starting my poems is that they're usually gotten into before the first light, just after night's-sleep and a little hypnopompic thought and some homely exercises and chores, with black cold instant coffee. Thus primed, I try to seek/allow some lines. No rush (not much). Also, I see, looking through recent mss., I start, or prepare to start (jot), upon having a thought, like "Those four (Gunnison) cottonwoods are both incredibly ragged and incredibly formal...." Open, I hope, to residues of clatter.

JC: Can you describe your workroom(s)?

LH: Here it is, extending 6 feet to my left, 18 to my right, 10 behind me, and in front of me just beyond the computer screen are four windows, one of which is open, looking out on the boughs of a redwood tree rooted in the neighbors' backyard and hanging over ours. Along most of three sides of the room runs what I suppose one would call a "work top," giving me about 9 feet of space, 27 inches deep, on which to spread papers and another 6 on which to work on "films" (mixed media drawings/collages). The late afternoon sun is shining on some black and white photos that I'll eventually cut into 1-inch squares for the "films"—I'd better move them, lest the light fade them. And the other (you suggest there might be two)? The other is here on my neck and teeming with thoughts, thick as milk in parts and thin as wisps of an infant's hair in others, moving like the images in a Brakhage film. Do you write down your dreams? Do you have any recurrent dream or recurring type of dream?

JC: I don't, except very rarely, write down my dreams. I think I "should," and have put pen and yellow pad by bed sometimes to facilitate same (the details evaporate so quickly—why is that? Simply because they lack the real-time anchors memory's chained to?) but haven't habituated myself to it. I think the transitive juice of dream is available (like verbs, or verbness, are available, I mean) during awake-time, perhaps more "purely" than if one organized dream representations. Many dream writings, in my opinion, are falsified by the scribes' focus on narrative and on symbolic "meaning." I think a better way to write dream would be to let the syntax catch the dream's atmosphere. I love to catch phrases from dreams—they seem like lines from a, say, Ted Berrigan poem. A recurring dream in childhood was of being on the rough, broken wall of a square ruin and being chased round and round on this wall by a large gorilla. Another was of a bear gradually lightening to my actual window as I opened my eyes. A young-adult image was of inching my way along an I-beam covered with tattered burlap high above a city both mysterious and "normal." And I visited this city again and again (a bit like a cross between Tripoli and Rome). I often dream of being caught in terrific complications with people. If you were beginning-college age again, what would you study that you actually didn't (much)? Discuss.

LH: Biology—botany, probably, or meteorology. Or both—you aren't asking me to imagine a career but only an epistemological adventure. And it would be that—every discipline occupies (or generates) its particular knowledge-ethos. When I was "beginning-college age," however, it was precisely "the ethos" of the sciences (as I, in my ignorance, understand it) that kept me from doing any more than fulfill the "science" requirement in place at Harvard (or Radcliffe, as it was for women until the year of my graduation—I have a "Harvard" degree but went to "Radcliffe"). Prior to that, in the all-girls school I attended, students had to take science every semester, but we were continually exposed to the notion that science was inappropriate for women. This was in the late 1950s—I graduated from high school in

1959—the era of what C.P. Snow called "the two cultures," the humanities and science at odds with each other. The idea that science was antithetical to the imagination prevailed—what a shame! I wish I'd studied philosophy, too (one can do so on one's own, but one is likely to remain an amateur), and Greek.

[....]

JC: If you were a taxonomist, would you be a "lumper" or a "splitter"?

LH: Truly fine taxonomy requires that one have the analytical skills of the splitter and the synthetic skills of the lumper, and I would, of course, want to practice truly fine taxonomy. I'd begin with the splitting—discovering the minutest distinctions so as to discover subsets among sets and subsets among subsets. I would delight in discovering veritable singularities. But then, having discovered the dissimilarities abiding between, say, very, very similar flying bugs that make some of them one sort of Pterygota, for example, and others another, I'd lump. I'd lump in the accepted way by gathering them with sow bugs, ants, and butterflies in the class Insecta within the Phylum Arthropoda, and I'd lump them with lobsters, such as the one that Jean-Paul Sartre thought was following him as he walked along the beach. I'd lump Sartre with Aristotle and split him from Camus. I'd lump the beach with my kitchen because sand from a beach is on my kitchen floor. Do you own any valuable furniture? Antique silver? First editions of 18th century books?

JC: No, no, and no. Jennifer does (own things of this kind). I own an old car and a tiny fraction of my old house. I do own a chair I like very much, made in Olathe, Colorado (it may have cost ten bucks). The seat is somehow a wild collage of polished wood fragments pressed into a square, like a sonnet about a hurricane. When we were in Olathe a week ago, I looked for the store in which I'd bought this chair (years ago while working there in Migrant Education). The store had been inside a hill of dirt, but I learned it had been torn down not long ago. I do own a couple shelves of '60s poetry books and booklets which could be worth a lot. I'll have to ask Steve Clay. If you had to be some other living person (than you are), who would you pick? Discuss.

LH: I'm not sure I like being myself, but I can't think who among living persons I'd prefer to be. Once inside the skin of someone, I'd be likely to find things just as uncomfortable or weird or difficult or complicated as they are inside my own. Being someone—anyone—entails all kinds of complexities, but at least I find this one (being myself) workable. I wouldn't dare take on the task of actually being even one of the people I most admire; they each seem more or less tormented, at least some of the time. In fact, the notion that one might suddenly be someone else is terrifying—like a key plot element in a horror film. Being no one is terrifying, too, of course—and that is a prospect we have to accept nonetheless, since that's exactly what being dead is. Do you agree with Gilles Deleuze that "it is the task of language both to establish limits and to go beyond them"?

JC: Yes. Thus language is seen as a living creature; limits are seen as relative; contradiction is seen as life's condition; reduction is seen as arbitrary. With language animal rather than machine, one climbs on (if one dares, if one cares) ready for a ride, not just a plan. Then the niceties of domestication/wildness come into play. The simultaneous action of both becomes possible ...

LH: How much revising (rethinking) do you do—and how much rewriting?

JC: "How much revising (rethinking) ... and how much rewriting" seems to break things along a line I'd like to blur. That is, type blurs, and amount depends. Lately it seems I could, given the energy, prophetably change every damn thing I've ever written. The degree to which I haven't focused hard enough, over mottled time, plunges sometimes clear up into a very puerile satisfaction with some instant gallop of the hand (about like this sentence). But I do love to tinker, and I tinker on tinkering's adrenalin when love is gone (or perhaps love = adrenalin), and I've learned that the cold light of morning isn't necessarily the last word. Bullets ...
- Policy: conscious decision, each typewriter space.
- Ideal: each part comes as a little vision.
- I used to think up steps more logically.
- I lie abed in the hypnopompic state, and then try to remember what slid in (even about revision).
- If it's musical it ain't all bad.

- Nothing is obvious but obviousness itself (i.e., originality isn't).
- Revision and cowardice did a little dance together. They talked a bit, tailed off; stepped on each other's feet; exchanged phone numbers (adjacent zip codes).

Is the fox ambitious because it knows what to do? The rain?

LH: Being neither an ethologist nor a meteorologist, I can't speak for the fox or the rain. Certainly the rain doesn't "know what to do" in the common sense; it "does" nothing, though it of course has enormous effect. Foxes do know what to do, at least insofar as foxiness is concerned, and no doubt they compete—but (non-human) animal competition is not clearly synonymous with "ambition." But then again ambition, in the human sense, seems not to mean what it once did; our word "ambition" comes from the Latin *ambitio*, meaning "going around," and certainly foxes do that. One synonym for "ambition" is "strong desire for advancement," and if we imagine the fox to be advancing toward food, no doubt it feels just that: a "strong desire for advancement." The rain may fall on this semantic field, but that's merely coincidental. The rain neither has nor doesn't have ambition. Do you think academic life is bad for a poet?

JC: It's not only bad, it's necessary. When I was on the brink of adult life (feeding myself), just post-Air-Force, I had to decide what to do, with poetry the number one concern: be academic or no. I decided it'd be too dangerous to my poetry to over-articulate my responses expositionally, as academics do. Workwise, I "went manual." Perhaps for too long. My poetic development has been slow. At some point (somewhat Colorado-isolated) I ran out of ideas of what to read next and went back to school (factory days, CU nights), so someone would tell me what to read. But this was all very patchy. I get very frustrated because I can't read, say, *Poetics Journal* 10. I should try harder. I think academic life at best gives understandings of work, time, and context. Multiplicity. Perhaps there should be a rule: academics spend 4 months teaching and studying, 4 months writing and studying, and 4 months laboring in factory, farm, or diner. Everyone should be academic (in a grove of trees, but not with Plato), because only a rare genius can be an autodidact and transcend mere crankdom. Because education takes you outside the self. Do you think academic life is bad for a poet?

LH: When I was a university student, New Criticism was in control of academic readings of poetry, and I thought they were awful, not because they were imposing "theory" or "interpretation" on the poetry but because they were excising poetry from the lived contexts out of which it developed. I rebelled accordingly and would have answered most emphatically "Yes!" to that question. But except for a moment just the other night, since the emergence of post-1968 "theory" and what's called "the turn to language," it has been possible again for "the academy" to be a site for the fulminating, debating, developing, and sharing of ideas. It has been so for me. And, to speak of it from another perspective, even if academic life were "bad" for the poet, the kind of work one does in (helping kids think and showing them great things to think about), it is surely something one can believe in. As for the moment of doubt I experienced "just the other night"—to tell the truth, I don't now remember what I was worrying about. It's true that I'm no longer isolated from "the mainstream"—which is to say, in the context of my work I do from time to time hobnob with mainstream poets, and I'm sufficiently polite (and insufficiently angry at *them*) to do so amiably. Perhaps I was worried that I had "lost my edge." I'm not worried about that right now. Wittgenstein, when he was teaching at Cambridge, encouraged—indeed insisted—that his best students "go manual." Several did (not very happily). Let me ask you one of Wittgenstein's questions: "Can one order someone to understand a sentence?"

JC: One can order someone to understand a sentence. Perhaps the "real" question Ludwig was suggesting with his interrogatory sentence was on the order of "May education properly include autocratic directives in regard to subject matter of great subtlety and sensitivity?" I say yes. I believe in the varied arsenal. I believe in "Just do it" in balance with enormous slathers of inveiglement. But I think he was suggesting, by putting the question, how ridiculous mere autocratics would be. He was spotlighting, or, more exactly, backlighting, the intricacy of the sentence, the impossibility of reaching a sole, perfect understanding of any sentence. Nuf sed. Should we (humans), in thinking of and planning for the future, match the time span of our considerations to the time span of our effects? (I.e., if the major effects of our presence on Earth reach roughly a thousand years down the road, should we so vastly increase the scope of our decision-making as to match that length of time?)

LH: Yes and yes again. But it's hard to believe that "we (humans)" (or "we contemporary first world humans") do much thinking and/or planning for the future at all, greedy predacious creatures that we prove ourselves to be. The best of us grieve over our times and litter, tossing drained bottles into the grass. Of course, the various religions of the world generally seem intent on reminding us of the meaninglessness of our desires and plunder, though some (like Christianity and, I think, Islam) insinuate that the meaning is just deferred to an afterlife, positing such a zone as one in which we reap the profits of our endeavors in life. But what does contemporary, secular, postmodern art have to say about what I'm calling "the meaningfulness" while meaning "the meaninglessness" of our desires and plunder? A few generations ago, an art of "the meaninglessness" was regarded as nihilistic, its message "carpe diem." A better message might be "salve diem"—save the day.

[....]

LH: How does one keep rats, raccoons, and opossums out of the compost?

JC: Probably a heavy or lockable lid on the compost container. I'll check with Jennifer.... Jennifer says (at first), "Why bother?" (if the compost's not too close to the house). She added, "Depends: where it is, the kind of pit. For homemade rigs, chicken wire works." I'll extend response to, say, Whitman, who posits a world of compost, a happy situation no matter who gets into it, with diseas'd corpses sprouting exquisite raspberries and the like. He wrote, however, about a status quo; now the larger composting of that seems underway (as it was then, invisible), and certainly saving the day contains living the day but not in such a way as to exclude raccoons. As for the rats, they depend on big water, and the possums, though spreading like kudzu, haven't got to the Continental Divide (which "Old Possum" retreated from, deserted). What do you do when plans get changed?

LH: I rethink the situation, re-cast my desires, I adjust—but not at first. At first I resent the changing of the shape of the day (whatever day it is that the plans pertain to), the changing of its contours (expansive at certain hours, restricted at others) and its rhythms (fast and slow), which I'd imagined and prepared myself for, with pleasure or with determination or with resignation. I'm reprehensibly stubborn. But wait—what kind of plans are you referring to? Do you plan out your poems?

JC: Sounds like Intelligent Design. I'd rather evolve them, but yes and no. Perhaps. Partly. Maybe I'll muster a rhythm; spot a slant; mostly I shoot for a slow spontaneous state (cold black coffee) and halfway trust it. But I like to make up grids, utilize gimmicks. The more meaningless/rigid the more I can groove with 'em. And then, ho hum, have to think about the world, etc. (as if I could). Seem kind to be kind. "Plan out" seems to connote basic start-to-finish calculation, but I just want to abstract preparatory thought enough to get going barefoot and then get concrete musically, which is abstract, not think up connections just have 'em. Then cut out "the" bullshit and hope there's not only something left but something which excess brevity hasn't butchered or made too "cool." Next age in the cask, take to task, re-do, see if it resembles a head of hair or what. Can you write a little biography of your hair?

LH: Yes. I wasn't born with much hair but in time it grew and in time what grew was plaited by my mother into two long braids whose tips I sometimes sucked. In time those were cut off and my father wept. For some years thereafter the hair hung at middling length and was sometimes clumsily rolled into curlers, producing blobs resembling earmuffs. When it was 18 or 19 years old, the hair was allowed to grow again, and my father who had wept when it was cut off now wished it was kept short. He said it was a mess. Sometime later he died. Periodically with a pair of tiny scissors I cut the split ends off individual hairs. Around 1987 it was cut short and "permed" and hidden (because the sudden change in its appearance embarrassed me) under a scarf, but it broke free and stayed curly until 1996, when it was all shaved off. Its life since then has been lackluster.

JACK COLLOM

First Letters to Each Line in "Introduction To Poetry"
by Billy Collins

I
a
l

o

I
a

I
a
w

B
i
a

T
t

—2006

silverb

leaf   10-30-89

In failing light—in fact—black-boled tree
no Preston would question, nor Daphne identify—hangs
onto hanging leaves (many are fallen), each turning
crisp—like an old hand—the color
of butter seen through dirty plastic—edges
ragged like a wild horizon ...

now plunge
through dirty window onto
yellowing oval
sliced ground value
surrounded
by sierras
land of belief

fantasy leaf
we walk boustrophedon
each pace
parabolic lace
infinite starlife with minuteman
strife
back & forth

to the black north polar
stem
& onto the black-boled
system like a
river in reverse
rippling seasons
& out

Necessary
processor of the light no doubt
(leaf)
in the shout of life, when growth is sweet and gross,
but now
snow's due.

each flake unique.

Love   Light   Landing   Lisping,
Enters   Eaten   Ends   Eternal
Air   And   Atmospheric   African
Force.   Fotosynthe-   Flicks.   Floor.
    sized.

Looming   Leftover   Lapland   Liquid
Edges   Emissaries   Endures   Elegance,
And   Almost   Atavistic   *Alte*
Flats.   Fly.   Firs.   *Frau.*

Lazarus   Language   Liberty   Labial
Eternalized   Emerges   Entails   Emerald
After   Amid   Action-filled   Attains
Falling.   Folds.   Failure.   Flap.

Lips'   Leaving   Let's   Literary
Entrance   Early,   Emulate   Echo-chamber's
Adduces   Anticipating   A   Atelier
Factory.   Frost.   Frog.   Falls.

sun water plate
or green, or the poem
of a circle

serious & bold,
these farmers only blush when
death is near

follow the bee,
leaf up, old boy, king
the victorious piece

there's a time
when whole ground is covered
& trees full

when the wind
blows, leaves start dancing like
numberless gutshot prisoners

"Nature's first green
is gold," said Frost, then
turned to crackerbarrel

various patterns of
death in the flames between
green & brown

the leaf cell
is—virtually beloved because of
its delicate lustre

turn over a
new leaf; turn over a
new leaf again

I'd just as
lief drop dead when I's
at my best

Snow of the year's cold fall.
Snow of the composing longevity.
Snow of Anno Domini, snow
of the New Stone Age, snow snow snow,
snow of the Pleistocene cycle.
Snow, simple white, simple black, simple newspaper wrapping
of the dead fish of the mote.

Ubi sunt Moby Dick?
Ubi sunt white verse?
Ubi sunt the all-reflecting past?
Ubi-sunt White Earth Syndrome, the whole
She-bang, the coming
of the New Year? Ubi sunt
white time bottleneck of the Big Black Bang?
& Ubi sunt the silver of the mirror?
Here it is late autumn.
Seasons're spreading in concentric circles;
nobody looks at them unless to say,
Where, pray tell, can I rake 'em away?

symbolic transfer scale to scale
(big wind)
(typewriter)
(sparrows in the branches)
(awkward pause)

The leaf introduces
light to the world. What does the poem
think of the leaf. The snow inside the face,
or the snow in common ears, or the snow of 200
(or the melting language of 1000) years, or the
snow that means any winter, when we think of
winter as a growth of white concentric
wraps. The poem wraps around the leaf.
Space wraps around the poem. The leaf and
poem are famous for death, because we follow
them. There are a thousand greens and
just one black. The leaf lives and dies
in different lights, that soak in, that
curl inward. Poem is shadow of, leaf is picture of.
The hand feeds the brain, fingers through
eyes. Brain is made of leaves. Discoverers
of dirt have gone from wave to dot to
string. The discoverers of talk have gone
from string to dot to wave. Leaf wins.

Verbs

To bake on the moon:
> Conestoga

To look like a piece of lettuce:
> Limpiarme.

To smash dolls:
> Hackenkreuz

To guard two paths at once:
> Duenna.

To sprinkle fairies on an entire country:
> Atchison-Topeka.

To slice lilies while smiling:
> Slivovitz.

To be muscular only in photos:
> Imagism.

To find an animal between savoir and faire:
> Christianity.

To think, "Absurd/ that's my Word."
> Malcontextualizing.

Two-Three-Two's

What if
creeks and scenic
railroads interbred?

—

Quondam referee
crumbles up a
mud pie

—

I love
Jenny because she's
human nature

—

Beanorilp magnus
ih slitchab lop
zye phlargg

—

aleph Molokai
my dear girl
let's milk

—

each time
I spy somebody
new mump

—

Atchison Topeka
& my room
with bottlecaps

—

Don DeLillo
scrapes mahogany but
aces polish

—

Do you
eek climb over
radio remembered?

—

I have
a brick which
is it

—

sliding Africa
wait a minute!
huh? huh

—

my mind
is a field
prefab wonky

—

coarse deal
harming conies much
of mulch

—

kill that
macaronic phiz diphthong
Momma Mae

—

I prefer
wisdom in chaos
temporarily blind

—

the moose
is almost invisible
but there

—

Nurse Death
have some coffee
itch medicine

—

easy acres
brewed of brown
ordinary slip

—

when it
was pure bird
awkward feathers

—

maybe cool
marginalia, maybe not
parrot heaven

—

Dream

Surely the sea for the deer browsing on the bluffs overlooking it belongs
With the sky
In the background of their beliefs (should they have them)
But for us adrift below with binoculars
We seem to draw it
Near and as nine pelicans fly
Low over the cast surface
North of the earth on which we're picnicking after wandering
Through the fog I remember
The Roger Williams Zoo—the veterinarian
Amid the dreamy elephants (they won't charge—don't we
Wish!) swinging their trunks and the humidity
In the monkey house
While we live
We can notice such things
Not always to remember them well
Grey and swaying
Just as some people jiggle their feet or twirl
Locks of their hair or toss in bed
To alleviate anxiety in ever smaller increments
To repeat
Patterns over time cover
Time
And again repeat
Just as a person might, working like crazy, day and night, to cover
The possibility that she isn't real
And won't get this work whose rules keep changing done
Without circumambulating the table on which it sits
Prowling in the purportedly relaxed but actually predatory
Manner assumed by cats
With intellectual momentum and psychological twists

That could be interpreted as prophetic
In retrospect far off and still to come
In the future towards which we're traveling faster
And faster in black
Then day again night again day
Again
Night the flapping of a black wing
Gaining velocity behind the jerking
Sun a streak of fire
The moon
A fainter fluctuating band over trees that grow, spread, shiver, and collapse
Mistily or dustily
Without a trace to my disappointment (I try to catch
Or create it) but everything's
Gone, whole histories
Like dreams sink into nothingness under
My eyes
There is a bakery—wow!—if I hurry
I can get rye bread and a dozen macaroons
And a blanket in Denmark
From a peasant painted by Pissarro
Who nursed the infant
Kierkegaard
At her good breast which she cupped in her strong pink green-veined
purple-shadowed haystack-yellow hand and hitched
When he was done then stuffed
Back where it belonged without doing any good
Or harm
To her sense of justice
Poised on canvas
Spread to the wind
With abandon

Nocturne

A woman is expressing sympathy with a television character who is weeping and trapped, she is attempting to scratch her way through a plaster wall and no one thinks to come to her rescue, as she dolefully frowns, it's an unresolved situation, but a woman *should* imitate the facial expressions of strangers in order to understand them though nothing's resolved even then, it's just a premonition of the feelings she's to have, as she has them, taken out of the world, from real actors, who have just shattered the windows of a new gray sedan parked in the sun in order to get air to a gasping dog mournfully pressing itself against the door on the driver's side—(sympathy requires terrific optimism—bravado—therefore paranoia—) and now enter a bank from which they each get money though their paychecks are no good, which should trigger a real crisis but everyone is as acquiescent as if they've completely misunderstood.

Already I regret having singled the woman out.

Fable

There was once a boy and he had a younger brother who was mournful
The older boy put a silver saddle on his horse one day and, mounting the
       horse, turned to the young and said, "Sam, you've won"
A thief hidden behind a tree nearby overheard this and said to himself,
       "By tomorrow at this time it will be I who have won," but he was
       mistaken as mournfulness cannot be acquired in a day

There was once a poor man who was hungry all the time
"How dare you? how dare you?" he shouted out the window to people
       hurrying to the shops on the street below
But experience of disappointment cannot be taught, and the people were
       deaf to his queries then just as they are now

There was once a sailor who had so many nicknames he no longer
       remembered what it was he should be properly called
He sat in the dark and gazed at the sea until his eyes ached and he
       wondered why the sea, though could be said to resemble an eye,
       never gazed back at him
But heroic efforts often fail, perhaps because emotion is often a poor
       teacher

There was once a princess who long yearned to go to sea but, as if she were
       disaster itself, she was banned from ships
"I'm no more dangerous than a mouse," she said one morning to the
       miller, who simply pointed to the baited mousetraps with which
       he protected the flour produced at his mill
Yes, restlessness is a characteristic of human existence and neither travel
       nor rapacity can exhaust it

There was once an astronomer who earned his living by promising glory
       to the king
On weekends he sat with his daughter doing math—"efficiency," he told
       her, "is best served by contemplation"
Now that was an excellent astronomer, and he is admired in pedagogical
       circles even today as a man who prepared for every lesson in
       advance

There was once a doctor who had a kind heart and long fingers and he
lived by himself in a room over a bakery
"Everyone likes you plump and warm," the doctor would say to each of
his patients, which was just what he heard the baker saying to his
muffins as he took them from their tins
And so we see that in the transition from writer to reader more and more
information is made available—that doctor was a rogue!

We are never the worse for our dreams, and a nightmare should not
always be taken as a sign of a bad conscience
Serenity can be achieved through fussiness (although probably only for
the fussy)
True justice is never abstract and should therefore not be blindfolded

That's what we can learn from these tales and from other tales too

Comedy

Our would-be sensitivities are social
They are the result of careful observation
Empathy

Say you see someone naked
Check out the webs
Ripple, finger, and jab the ribs

Jiggle the ribs
You laugh?
How did we get to juggling pigs?

Elegy

The sky above is blue today—but not very blue
She's been knocking marbles around in the mouth, rolling them along
the teeth, pulling them back with the tongue
She was one who would refuse to be misled by bad data
E appears more often than T, T more often than A, A more often than I[1]
And the tiny gray garden spiders no bigger than a grain of sand with a
        bright dot of yellow on the back and white knobs to their
antennae, the earthworms that emerge
Man train seeks where she alights
There is nothing to prevent
Just as it is possible for A to attach to B so it is possible for C to attach to D
The one runs into the sea, the other runs from it
Georgette said seven avocadoes were required for the guacamole
Heart (absolute), readers (several), water (acts), another (recognized), view (dash)
Whatever happened to the gingerbread
A landscape has endless false endings
A cistern of water is hidden under the yard of my daughters—who am I

---

[1] John Lyons, Semantics I (43)

JACK COLLOM / LYN HEJINIAN

Collaborative Poems

Wicker

Let one line
of our poem
contradict
another!
(Walt Whitman)

secrets, sequences
the poem better
haunted by its rocks
let's speak of night, thought
an outlaw species

One secret of
our sequence
is another.
(U.S. Grant)

when there's
an outlaw species
what laws can it
press from thought to night?
and rolling downhill

I notice that
there is no
crescendo in our
narrative.
(Marina Tsvetaeva)

without looking
and rolling downhill
to kill until tomorrow
the sleepers curl and still
these night thoughts

(The red throated loon
dives.)

roll on
these night thoughts
curve over a mass,
a species breaking from a
trough of numbers

I'll make a thousand
celestial observations
and render their
seeming eccentricities
consistent for ever.
(Victor Frankenstein)

audacity's a
trough of numbers
a chaos still precise
if we've time to think
of watching unawares

Until the rise of modern
dentistry (enabled by drugs)
most denizens had nothing
to smile with, or above,

the root
of watching unawares
when "what-kind?" yellows
"anyways"

and those who just up and
smiled anyway … idiots.
(Edward Dorn)

    […]

& the main thing is
we begin with a white
sink a whole new language
is a temptation.
(Bernadette Mayer)

    […]

Which you can
when a moment's gone
for all I care.
(Josephine Baker)

Oh! penetrating to the
point of pain I fill
the depth of the sky
with consternation!
(Charles Baudelaire)

But then
everything cools out
again.
(Werner Heisenberg)

I fall into
the icy water, not
humiliated but
silenced
(Aphra Benn)

You gotta slide into
third as if you're
setting out to bury
yourself.
(Muddy Ruel)

is the quote the whereabouts
appears to broach

surpassed by
incongruity to be
taller than I when
I (or my equivalent) jut
elbow against tree

along the
decry the war
and the war's breath
that pushes until no atom
of absence remain

the ghouls
of absence remain
flickering in black and
white to make a show
of lifelike expressions

but cars
of lifelike expression
cruise the lines; one
flicker, then another, taps telephone
poles, translation overload

downs the
poles, translation overload
girds the white circles
to get the same smile
as marks thought

parenthesis, dash
as marks thought
with greasy red strokes
and one second of trickery
ghouls of absence

The Wonder

Great as the delicate sense of the flagrant fullness of any wondrous
Ladder's sketchy arrangement of space might be, the
Avaricious dreamer heading downtown on a bus at 8
Doesn't stand a chance of pure continuation, partly,
Let's imagine, because of breakdown or construction, the always only
        partly arbitrarily
You are there, you blew it, type of

Thing. Of course Picasso marveled one way, Trotsky
Ha muerto un otro
Eternally remarking (because he wrote it) "Well, and how about butterflies?"

"Mariposas?" murmured a voice at his side, even after
Interest in Nabokov's blues had peaked (everyone having both read
        and seen *Lolita*).
"Caríssima," muttered Leon, "I have an uneasy feeling about that man who
        calls himself Schmetterling
Rapidly and regularly and with utter disregard for the wonders that only he,
Ocularly speaking, obtains." "You're panting," she observed, placing
Silver coins on a lemon, and the wonder is they turned
Coppery red, or green. It was difficult to tell due to the iridescence that seemed
        to
Offset the warmth emanating from the flames. We huddled together wearing
        linen coats
Pleated in a wonderful series of half-hidden pictures
Inserted into the windswept fields of color of a wondrously clan-defying plaid.
Seersucker? No—I wonder … maybe woodpecker design, or camouflaged
        woodpecker
Tattersall resembling Nebraska or birchbark or a tiled kitchen wall in colors
        that seemed vaguely Provençal.

So wonderfully warm we were that when Lorrain offered to paint coats on us
In patterns replicating the dappled shadows cast by the leaves of the old birch
        tree we agreed as long as she used watercolor and only green-
Gage plums, sliced lengthwise, were served, under the birch tree, during the
        process.

Hilary was put in charge, having little to do but read fairytales to the children
     by day and dance, when they napped, with the Nigerian doctor,
The one who had memorized *Ulysses* and would recite it to his patients in lieu
     of anesthetics. He
Said that he found writers cruel, as cruel as pilots, who whisk one away and
     then land the plane

As if it were a tube of toothpaste simply being plopped on a shelf by a musical
     young woman hurrying off to work
Roguishly with her viola under her chin and the rights of women to defend
Education tucked under her belt, in apparent violation of the

Magnificent scientific discoveries that, under a pseudonym, she's made
Available to humanity on the condition that they not be entirely understood as
Gynecological. The wonder of the gamboling boys in view is that they'll dare
     to care to dare to gamble
Needlessly and heedlessly, and therefore for their right to roll up
Instinctively at nightfall after eating to dream of imperious winds and boats
Flying across monster-studded oceans, and the most bloody-minded monster
     of all
Is me! says the microscopist, setting his sights on a political career
Even though he wonders how many votes a sketchy arrangement of space
     might get
Delivered before the amazing day on which his happiness will be judged, his
     fate known.

Shims

Blatant
pattern through
shrinking and expanding
unfinished tapestries, show yourself!

A child's inbound anxieties
roll together like
outbound hostilities
aerodynamically

Soup?
for two
or even four
stands hot in bowls

Everything false falls away
as Earth's crust
shakes ferns
(yo-di-láy-ee!)

Quick
as rivals
neutrality and light
improve hindsight, disprove prophecy

Somewhere east of Java
suggesting it's suggestive
western sounds
subtitle

In the thick of
standing wave clouds
political thought
condenses

Kindergarten
implies weeding
W and X-ylophoning
which wind up WAX

Elmer's "yellow streak" showed
in milky glue
no matter
free

Freud
looked in
trepidation into her
dream of dandelion fluff

Preoccupied by big themes
the mother bear
sniffs air,
hesitates

Ditty-mongering
growl Hopis
there're mourning loops
Second Mesa pure yellow

When
suddenness's becalmed
some snakes assume
coils—spring's attentive étude

But close-dancing is so
perpendicular to desire,
my dear
wind

Warren
winding, porous
but scarcely harmless
harbors our inexcusable habits

In Albuquerque she found
the vertical sun
everywhere, even
gradual

Iodine
forted animal
in neglected sandstone
works the minimal unbrokenly

Orange edges around stark
widening winter-wizened projections
with sexy
fringes

Utopian gravel's spreading out
woodchuck light condenses
sour chalk
bingo

Credulity
settles it
—skepticism under silt
crumbles just like that

Remotely a blur (mirage,
then not) become
an impediment
hit

Ill-sorted
lawyers lay
bastion beside brevity,
emerged with pure basalt

Crescent oxen given walk
arrive with milk
from manuscripts
(metaphorically)

Impassioned
fast brown
greens up querulously
forming a dense bed

THOMAS SAYERS ELLIS

Spike Lee at Harvard

Five Joints

At the Grolier, I was
the shipping clerk,
employed in a corner
slim enough for a book.
I was surrounded by books,
by boxes of books,
and photographs of poets
and by customers
who loved poetry;
and by famous poets
who were also customers
and that is where
I got my first glimpse
of the life of poetry
(through the Grolier's
cinematic glass window)
and where the life of poetry
first governed me,
toward discipline and surrender,
to work through
a mandate of silence,
so as not to "take advantage"
of my "position,"
as if any black person
would want to use
shipping and sweeping
to create an audience
for apprenticeship.

The Grolier's interior
was all literary integrity
and repetition, as if lit
by the alliterative gaze
of illiterate, lettered spirits,
its own elite enemy
of non intellectuals
and integration. "Should we
separate the black poets
from the white poets
to make it easier
for customers to find
African American work?"
My employer asked,
well, at least she asked.
One part of me thought,
"What's wrong with
this white woman?"
And the other part
… thought, "Hell No!"
but all I said was,
"I   don't   think   so,"
… said it slowly, so
as to suggest
the lyrical range of attitude.
Another, mo betta, way
to frame this is to say that,
then, there was only
one black poet
on the wall of photographs,
Ai, interrupting
the white typeface
of American detachment.
A single profile of personas
like a caesura
in buttermilk.

A sonnet surrounded
  by the shadows of ideas
and knives of artificial light,
the Grolier was
day for night
for nothing
but their work
and their likeness,
the colorless absence
of noise between
images and words.
Shelving was like casting;
being up on the ladder
like directing, all perspectives
of craft mine to theft.
Yes! Letterpress chapbooks,
signed overstock,
folded broadsides. *No!*
Of all the books I'd stolen,
I'd never stolen from The Grolier,
but you would not
have known that
from the auctioneer's way
she moved through my work,
like an apparition of inventory,
chained to suspicion.
Three times around
the center display table,
under which Pumpkin
the shop's dog slept,
was like one time around
Ben Hur's Coliseum, in
Hulot's hiccupping jalopy,
as publishing, like
the Gulf War, filled
the world with
more ghosts.

In my other life,
    I was given an audience,
the keys to darkness,
an office of shadows,
and an editor's sense
of control over
my own crew of light.
Forgive me, champions
of Identity Politics,
for not just saying:
I had an evening job
as a projectionist-security guard
at the Harvard Film Archive,
in the last line
of Le Corbusier's
ramped prose poem
of glass and stone,
whose screen, like big paper,
was wide as the sky
and less restricted
than the Grolier's
marquee-like anthology
where the white people
in the framed photographs
rejected the glamour
of the white people
in movie stills.
My favorite being the photograph
of Gordon Cairnie,
the shop's original owner,
and Louisa Solano,
his young assistant,
locked in their
own couplet
for final cut.

As auteur, as author,
   I pray this last stanza
won't fade or break
into whiteness, the tense silence
at the end of rioting.
Down there, in the sync
between thinking and feeling,
this is where the soundtrack
would begin if poetry
paid enough for one;
if the public paid
more for poetry.
Dear Listener, are you
as swole by this as I was living it,
these five different takes
of the same sickness?
Already, you must
be tired of these uneven
four, five and six word lines.
If so, toss a trashcan,
like a lidless metaphor,
through this poem's
narrative, wild style
into the sepia flashback
of any number of book parties.
For every insult
and broken promise,
the crash, a critical review,
the flying glass.
Poets running
for cover with nothing
to cover themselves
but their own book covers.
Call the cops if you like.
Their slanted shadows
can't spell a hold
on craft.

No Easy Task

Suddenly our names
were more than our own,
our dramas too. And,
as if the craft of our
inherited calling had only
two camps of Blackness,
"Academic" and "Spoken Word,"
our best work, the work
for all work, had to work
on the page (if we wanted
to be published) and
on the stage (if we wanted
to be recorded) ... but, mostly,
we just wanted to be whole
(respected and known) and
heard (reviewed and enjoyed)
as in In the tradition of "worriation"
and "... a loud noise followed
by many louder ones."
And not always as lonely as an "I"
and not always as burdened as a "we"
and never anyone's token,
hyphen, bridge, honorary anything,
or literary pet ... even if
the listeners weren't reading
what we were scribbling
and the readers weren't listening
to what we were spitting ... even if
an Open Mic never opened
an open book, *haters,*
and an opened book
never booked an Open Mic,
favorites. An ironic browbeat
if you a sonnet. If you a star
you wish you were higher,

a sermon. Enter audience,
the audio antithesis
of academia, worrying
text to talk and talk to text.
How ... entertainment, poor folk-prosody,
oral jewelry, flow? The problem
with American poetry
is there's not enough Africa
in it; bling-bling has more
rhythm and imagery
than all of Ashbery.
At the edge of subjects,
poetics. At the center
of subjects, prose.
The uneven ribs of verse,
with its progression
of resurrections, reverses.
Out-dated show-offs
like villanelles and sestinas,
pretending not to perform,
costume form. The content
of character, not the shape
of content, shapes form.
There's no such thing
as formlessness. *Applause.*
All poems perform.

Schema

He was born as his name implies
as though distortion weren't enough
in itself to frighten good, innocent people.
Even little children utter bold words,
but that's not the half.
There remains an apology that is due.
      How necessary it is we keep secrets.
And what is to be done
to prevent something awful from happening—
or perhaps we just get used to it.
If momentum can do so much,
just imagine what it will do for us.

Signs of Good Humor

The little room
is always a little
dirty. The frozen north
we take to be a plain
statement of fact. Pre-
formulated as the backdrop
good humor erupts
puzzling over
the question as to
why in the house
of dread, cleverness
and strangeness, however,
are acknowledged
with gratitude—
a brilliant light as from
a calcium in a theater
beats upon the far
corner of the domicile.
The sense of space
and loneliness upon
the sea is all I get.
From an upper
window a woman
instead of focusing
bends, her tumbling
hair only sufficient—
only sufficient touches
the troubles of a man
and woman and the calcium
light upon the house
scarcely awakens
my interest.

His Blood Be on Us

Since the times seem out of joint for a correct definition,
or even a proper gathering of facts, let us pray for all
the items we should like to have. Except for cleverness
it's all over. He just slipped & slipped with timidity
finer than strength. Like a brazen carbon the intent
is satiric but effective in a dim room. I'm amused
you should feel in the calm of the quiet of Sunday
morning a sense of something strange hanging over you.
The idea here is unmistakable, given a fixed set
of circumstances and a certain individual end. In the end
it is a poor romancer who cannot work out the result.

The sky is excellent. In a neighboring landscape
two young women in extravagant white finery
enter a once notorious dance hall. Gratitude alone
should compel us for what now in the blue weather
shows signs of becoming settled. He has come to us at last.

The White House

He knows how to do what he sets out to do

                      with perfectly obvious procedure. The sea

                      is dark and forbidding. The horizon

                      is dark and forbidding.

Even from a distance, the less said the better. The colors in some of

                      these landscapes are perfectly desperate.

In a portrait there is never anything wrong

                      with the mouth. There is never anything wrong

                      with anything. Machines are not choosers.

                      The next best things are certain. Heaven

                      knowing the next best things. The young

                      can explain it, but who would they explain

                      it to? More promise than performance

                      as all sorts of things begin to interfere.

An energetic hostess seated me at the counter

                      next to a beautiful woman. It is possible

                      the timid portion of the population

                      unless held firmly in check will imitate

                      the silliness of timid people of years ago.

Supplication is valued. As soon as I learned the facts I gave up

                      on the exchange. She wanted something

                      mysterious, as if everything were the same.

Life changes and so-called "truth" changes with it. The businesslike

                      haste of the surgeon as he scolds the public.

                      To look at him and the thing he can never look at

                      shudderingly as the blood is drawn

                      is the duty of every patriot.

In a constructive age such as this I should have neglected everything
                        for the supreme duty of aiding
                        in the reconstruction.

I took my courage which starts everywhere and goes
                        nowhere and spoke to her. Here
                        one can unquestionably infer the inside
                        from the outside.

The leaders of the free world, assembled as if by magic,
                        seem to have the enemy at their mercy.
                        It can be argued that Christ himself spoke
                        to the mob. The crowd will stop
                        to see almost anything. The crowd will stop
                        to see something about almost everything.

ESMAIL KHO'I

from Persian by Niloufar Talebi

To the Aged Mulberry Branch

A long string
Trails
To a torn kite
      Hanging
From a branch of an aged mulberry tree
Whose afternoon umbrella of shade
Spans over the hubbub of the barefoot children of the alley

My goodness!
My entire childhood—
Summer-like—
Caught in the snapshot of this memory!

Look:
Dusty earth,
     Dusty sky,
          Dusty sun
And dusty children
Picking up dusty mulberries
        With dusty hands
From dusty earth
                    To blow on
                      And place

in their mouths!

And a torn kite
On the branch of an aged mulberry tree …

Losing

I was a handsome springing fish
At youth's waterfall
        But
                My space
                        Was cramped
                                For me.

My Space
        In the waterfall?
                No:
                        Inside my fair self,

Space
        Was too tight
                For me.

I wanted to
        Rise out of myself
To make
My world fairer than myself.

Do not ask me
Who I am,
Or what I am,
Or what I am doing in your desert hearts.

I do not remember when,
                How,
                    Why,
                        But

I wanted to
Rise out of myself.

MINA ASSADI
from Persian by Niloufar Talebi

Yearning for Saari (1)

Oh you wet weeds,
      that grow on the riverbanks of my homeland,

tell the breeze
      that so lovingly passes through you
            that someone on this side
                  of the world is also enamored
                      of the scent of your bodies.

Saari is a region in Northern Iran

Waking Dreams (3)

Had they lasted,
they would have blossomburst—
the almond trees

                  that escaped the axe.

Had they remained,
      the children's mouths would have brimmed
                        with ripe nectar of
almond

and even with
bitter almonds—
        had they remained.

Waking Dreams (6)

After rain
        there will be rain

After loneliness
loneliness

After you
        a silence
                that shall give new meaning to loneliness

After night
        there will be night

After nightmares
        nightmares

After you
        a silence
                that shall give new meaning to my nightmares

Because of Boredom

Grant all the desks in the world
                                to the man
                                        who writes
                                                but is not a poet.

And in return,
                give me a cool glass of water
                                        to put up
                                                with his existence.

Winter in Mt. Auburn Cemetery

The linen-colored light spreads through the great,
mortified fingers of the European Beech.

When what has been given away does not return,
light reflects from the gravestones, as if they were stars.

Think of all the people this landscape has taken
into its mouth and held like wafers of dust.

And yet it aches with want. Like people gone blind.
But in this pain there is silence, occasional

flutter of blackbirds, the sky an exacting shell of blue.

HENIA & ILONA KARMEL

from Polish by Fanny Howe

These poems were written by a young woman of twenty and her sister of fifteen in the forced labor camps of World War II. Henia and Ilona Karmel were born into an affluent and distinguished family in Krakow. They spoke Polish, Yiddish, and German. They read Hebrew and Western classics as well as Adam Mickiewicz and the contemporary Polish-Jewish poet Julian Tuwim.

"Let me try to sketch for you the Polish Jews as I knew them in my youth," Ilona Karmel wrote years later. "A heterogeneous world of city dwellers who lived in a complex and tragic contact with the non-Jewish community. Yet, be it because Polish society would not accept them; be it because they would not have felt at home in it, they remained intensely Jewish; seeing their hope in Zionism and, out of a kind of visceral loyalty, observing the Jewish customs ... Then came the war. And even the assimilants, those believers in the ultimate acceptance of Jews by the Gentile world, had no illusion about the forces that barred the way to acceptance. 'Poland without Jews'—this was the atmosphere of the thirties. The first evils of the Nazi occupation; the armbands with a star of David, the closing of Jewish schools and stores were therefore painful yet not shocking.... It was the continuation of a familiar trend rather than a new development."

At that time 60,000 Jews were living in Krakow and many immediately escaped to Russia and elsewhere. Declared Jews were forced to leave the surrounding villages, a scene described in Henia's short story, *The Last Day*, published years later in the emigre magazine *Kultura*, and later reprinted in *The Best American Short Stories, 1962.*

Throughout 1942 conditions in the Krakow ghetto continued to grow desperate, with deportations and murders emptying the population day by day. People who remained were held there to work in slave conditions, while the Germans constructed the concentration and labor camps in nearby rural areas. Plaszow, where the Karmels would be sent, was built on two Jewish cemeteries.

For a time Ilona worked as a cleaning woman to a German family in Krakow and smuggled food back to the camp to share with others. Henia worked in an ammunitions factory for eight to twelve hours a day without food or the milk that would cut the effects of the toxins on their bloodstream.

There was continual resistance from inside the barbed wires, and it was here that many of these poems were written. A non-Jewish worker in the plant gave Henia and Ilona extra worksheets to write on. These sheets were handed in to the boss at the end of every day, but one side was blank. It was on these blank worksheets that the poems were composed in pencil (also very difficult to get hold of) and then concealed. There was an invention of cultural life at this camp, really a form of reminiscence, that included prayer, drawing, song, poetry—all with references and sources instantly recognizable to those present.

In a section of Buchenwald set aside for women, Henia and Ilona still had the poems with them—sewed into the hems of their dresses. And long afterwards survivors would remember the two sisters reciting them, Henia's voice being particularly memorable for its musical quality.

How these poems came to be read again, outside the camp and the war, is a story in itself that began with the forced evacuation of Buchenwald. When the SS sent prisoners on forced "death marches" nearly 28,000 prisoners were forced by the Germans to walk in circles through the roads and forests outside the camp and in this process, many of them were crushed by Germans in tanks and shoved into a pile. Henia and Ilona and her mother were three of these. They were pushed into a field of corpses and abandoned. Ironically, because their blood was so thin from starvation, they managed to stay conscious. A Polish woman who had been working as a slave laborer in a nearby farm, came upon the heaps of corpses, and by chance saw that some people were alive. This was how Henia, Ilona, her mother and a Hungarian woman were driven by horse and cart to a nearby hospital where there was only one doctor left.

In the hospital the sisters each had a leg amputated and their mother who had stayed with them throughout the years died there.

Sweden was known to offer the best treatment in rehabilitation and Henia and Ilona eventually moved to a hospital there. They stayed there for the next two years where they continued to write poetry.

I met Ilona Karmel on our first day of work at MIT in the fall of 1978. We were friends from that moment on. We shared books, mostly theology and philosophy, and talked about personal history, about matters that were very specific to two people born in the heart of the twentieth century. The poems included here are rough, immediate, emotionally young and determined by early education in rhymed verse. The two sisters used traditional forms which helped them preserve a learned and beloved culture in the midst of its destruction. And while these forms had already been abandoned by many modernist poets in Eastern Europe, they served a purpose for these prisoners. They were produced in that stretch of time in the twentieth century when something that couldn't happen, did. The poems express what it's like to dwell at the center of an anti-miracle.

I have discovered—in working on these poems—something I never fully understood before; poetry seeks the impersonal and translation can actually advance that search. When you work with the literal version of a poem that was written in a language you do not know, the texture of syntax alone, as material sound, is all you have to go by. It is the words alone that excite the next words; it is like geometry. I could lift a word that was in the original in one place and take it to another place in the poem and the same poem would be standing in position. An adjective that sat against one noun might find itself against another noun, so that the translation was finally concentrated in single words rather than on fully established sentences. How they emotionally added up and were accounted for musically was my driving concern. Most often this meant reducing rather than expanding the language. Just as a person longs to act freely in a way that supercedes even intelligence (and these gratuitous acts were in fact the only acts that came to interest Ilona in her life and her fiction) there is something of this stretch towards the impersonal gesture in the translation of poetry. However, I realized that "adaptation" was a more precise word for the process I had gone through; while the translators had translated from Polish to English,

I had adapted their translations to the poetics of the period in which they found themselves. Animals adapt to new territories. Poems do too. Animals are adapted from the wilderness to the barn by the farmer. Poems are adapted from their original source by a poet in a new place.

In all poetry rhythm and corresponding sounds (even among letters) are echoes of each other. The labor of writing seems to cut the suffering; in this case utterance stands for each sister's personal will to live while in prison. A prisoner recently released from the prison in Guantanamo said he wrote poetry to keep his sanity; the words of his poems are remarkably similar to those in this volume. There is the same limited experience that has unlimited consequences. What keeps coming through to me from the Karmel sisters' verse is an oracular voice, as if the stones or the earth had found speech. What is there, as Beckett might put it, is a mouth as much as a voice.

An Answer

How can I act so calm?
Strangely in prison rebellion is quiet.
Days are like sleep.
You are of a piece with the machines.
A screw that turns one way only.
Honestly, I've lost any sense
Of purpose or meaning.
I'm calm because of this.
But it doesn't bode well.

I have no belief and no desire,
No expectations.
I'm like a spectator
Who is not present at her own life.
In the end, I'm just plain tired.
That's all. My calm comes
From being forsaken by all.
It doesn't bode well.

—*Henia Karmel*

The Demand

I have something to say to you.
It's grim, outrageous.

I don't want happiness or peace
From this world.

No, not while eternity burns inside of me.
Raw and violent with stars
And days bursting and recreating.

I feel it.
I am young and passionate.

Don't let my heart break!
Let it stay strong
Enough to carry me on.

I want to wander
With my longing and my hurt too.
And even if I am slowed by pain
I still want to seek the truth.

—Ilona Karmel

Verses

I bet you're thinking *Not more poetry!*
You might even add,
Please, even if they're not the worst ever.

But guess what? This isn't verse at all.
It's made with the ink of tears.

God has sent down a spell
And a wall and every word
Inside is cursed.
This is not poetry. It's an alarm bell.

It's a scream, a thunderburst,.
Syllables in a rush.
The same old sounds
You always hear but now insane.

The universe is distressed
When no one knows how to say things fresh:

"Sorrow, reverie, lamentation, dream,
Chaos, wilderness, ruined youth,
Disease and desire
For help or revenge...."

That's the kind of poetry that this is.

—*Ilona Karmel*

Bread

I would love to have a loaf of bread.
Big, white and only for me.
The whole thing.
Fresh, hot and smelling of caraway seeds.
A crunchy crust
Brown and crackling.

And to bite in with my teeth and chew
Caressingly, blissfully bite after bite,
Against the roof of my mouth.
And finally to feel it heal and comfort
My empty stomach's
Unending appetite.

—Henia Karmel

Pears

A storm—a wind—the pears knocked down
Onto the morning street. Now look—
Despondent women—locked in formation.

See how furtively they stop
To pick up the pears from the ground and eat.

Even their guard—a decent old man—
Is ashamed to see their joy and greed.

—Henia Karmel

To My Friend

It is winter.
What more is there to say?
It is what it was when we were still alive.
And where did you disappear to?
And your eyes that I loved?

I keep looking at you
To calm myself down—
At your photograph, that is—it once made me cry.
I, un-alive, am writing to you who went away.

Yes. It is winter.
The frost is as strong as alcohol.
If I could just get drunk on it!
But then why bother? I'm drunk
On sorrow, and as low as the dusk.

I wonder if you remember
Snow-covered fields
And mountains swirling under clouds
How the earth becomes indistinguishable
From the sky.

The borders disappear as before.
The earth is as it was
When we were still alive.
Why did we believe, stupidly, that the sun
Would shut off and the world stop

When we were out of it.

No, it is as it was.
Dawn, dusk, etcetera, people who laugh
And cry, bless, curse, don't notice you left.
And I do the same, almost.

I'm writing this on a frosty day.
Halfway to you. The world slips through
The window via human voices.
Long beyond the range of my thoughts.
Snow, earth-line, very far away.

—Henia Karmel

The Origin of a Poem

First there is a soul and a seed
Swelling, secret, deep.
A troubled premonition.
Dusk, germination.

The seed is sharp, patient,
It spreads into words,
Strophes, sound, branches.
Then you are its gardener.

Its rhythm comes like a gale
That sways in your soul.

Your pen is your shovel
Transplanting these words
Into ridges on paper where
They flower in air, tear off and disappear.

—Ilona Karmel

Life Drawing

Youth

Hush. Close your mouth.
Raise your hand
Into a clenched fist.
This is youth.
Another story altogether.
Bitter and sad
Hard and unavoidable.

These memories won't quit.
They even hurt.
It was the autumn of '39.
How describe (in what language?
Fire?) that time.
When she arrived, she, youth,
She, without romance,
Or poetic introductions.
Distant reader, she came
With thunder, soldiers,
Cannons, machine guns,
Youth. No more fables.

I see the dark ditch and us in it.
Overhead, horrible wings.
Shock, screams, smoke, sun
And a shaking ground.

What was The World to us
Crashed down. Gray petals
Of smoke unfurled
Into a red conflagration.

From that moment on,
It would always be the same.
A mother's terror

And still her comforting hands.
Both of these, and that avalanche.

Time staggered forward
Without mercy
Carrying each person with him.
I grew from fifteen to sixteen.

The days were voracious,
Like creatures that clawed
At whatever we took with us.
The closest, the most loved.

They clawed until they dug
A horrible void into
Our childish faces!
We grew old, dull-eyed, dry.

Only hate stayed strong.
Little, but quite sufficient
To get us through the graveyard days
And give us more bitter knowledge.

The art of the closed fist
The clever closed fist.

Don't scream from pain.
Don't express rage.

Cut from your lexicon
The words happiness, laughter,
And change love to hate.
Words that would be a waste.

The simple and difficult art
Of self-censorship is to ensure
That no heart exists.

Mother's hands, once capable
Only of arranging flowers in a vase,
Were now hard, she learned
How to deflect a blow with them.

Love made them tough
While her face grew yellow,
Her eyes lost their life,
Until her heart gave up the struggle.

So friend, that is all
I can remember. You count.
How many graves? How many days?
It is now 1945.

Blood, a taste of morphine,
Bad dreams, no more mother's hands …

This is the epilogue, friend.
From my life inside four walls.

I have no childhood dreams, only
Visitations from the fearful
Nightmares of those years.

Worse for being known
But now with nowhere to run
For comfort from them.
No maternal hands.

The story ends here
When I am twenty.

—*Ilona Karmel*

ILYA BERNSTEIN

* * *

When the mystery of the crossroads was swept up
And incorporated into a man,
His soul became a parting of the ways,
His memory became a triple road.

A light that seems to come from far away
Points straight at me across the evening hour.
All for a crossroads, what have my bones become?
Oh, how inflexible is human flesh!

The future crunches underfoot, like gravel and sand.
And trees of dust stand out in the sun.
You know: two highways run across this world
And it requires something like a hand
To capture their intersection, like a bird,
And to install it in the ribcage of a man.

* * *

Who can say in advance what kind of liberty
The land will remember in a century?
Let the inhabitants proclaim their laws
And fling their lives against the dying day.
They shall discover, then, what a mountainside knows
About invariance and broken chains.

The nails are driven in and human beings
Divide the memory of freedom among themselves—
Through the richness of the soil,
Through tangled bare branches and the rising of the grass—
They lean on those divisions in their labor
Through the rule of law and openness to risk.

I know the written word and the spoken word.
They grind each other like cement and steel.
Find out that friction where liberty is stored
And put your faith in abstract things.
We live in the convergence of two wakes—
Virginia and Massachusetts are far away—
And the horizon grows, as they slip out of sight.

GIAN LOMBARDO

Keyed
to E

Clasped by clefts bereft of depth. Clueless in geyser.
The wet dry the wet.

Wherein the snake chases its tail to the signature
of two skins rubbing. (Which? Where?) The dry
wet the dry.

Resigned to pauses wherein each has drawn a
face gasping for the intervale's intervals.—Mud
muddies mud.—

Cease susurration. Turn not a blind eye to the
embargo of the loudest for they flower in earnest
and waver a lot.

P Can't
Intro P

Up to. But never beyond. No matter how hard. No matter. Just energy. No matter how critical.

Mass never reached. Perpetual hand out. Supple supplicant just one fricative short of complete enunciation. No matter however fissile.

Culmination's not incumbent but frittered the wrong way worn one rub shy of incendiary delight.

Half-Full
Circle

What could be more necessary than a sunspot? Let us choose a crab and a bagpipe since they accompany a straight line.

The bizarrest of equations laugh and elude the harshest daylight. Ask me what is foisted on grammar and thereby challenge the shortest shadow.

Soil grasps the falsity of what economy rejects. Phantoms reject sound digestion for the right to reverse happiness.

Profit merely a joke, let us breed from left to right. My finger points to knees if I read what emerges from a straight line as a loss of thirst.

When does the ascending line succumb to undeniable tyranny? Fundamentally, as long as good things wish to be read.

For even the sternest problems rejoice in a return to the soil.

Undue Attachments
to the Chimeric

It is known that asymmetries do not appear to be inherent. The customary view draws sharp: No properties correspond to absolute rest. Light, independent of emitting bodies, lies at the root of moving bodies.

Let us take a system. To describe the motion of a material point. Let there be a stationary rigid rod. Imagine further two ends. Imagine further a moving.

Let us take two systems. The constancy compatible. Be propagated from reasons of symmetry now evident.

Following peculiar consequence under otherwise identical conditions, empty space will hold good. If we call the moving system, light must appear.

A light complex seeks the pressure of light on a reflecting surface after reflection.

Let there be motion taking the ordinary point of view, motion resulting from system. This expression applies to ponderable masses, complete expression by which the electron must move.

The War on Terror

Satellite beaming
on the rose-
twined cottage:

no chains required
when slavegirl's
in the mood.

Only your birthright
for a mess
o' pottage,

and a barrelful
of sweet,
light crude.

Lapland Not Actually the Country of Lesbians

The country of lesbians
isn't Lapland, actually,

because unlike
Lapland, lesbianism

is a tundra of hooded
rosette lichen

not to be trifled with
by those who

don't herd the reindeer
of its crisp implacable

demands. The winds
of lesbianism blow

snow into the parkas
of those who don't

trudge under the Aurora
Borealis of

Lapland. I say this
even as I accuse myself

of pining after both
the bracing rigors of an

Arctic of lesbianism
and the blue lights

of the Lapp woman's
ice hut, her salty kiss

and the tickle
of her fur-lined bonnet.

AMELIA ROSSELLI

from Italian by Jennifer Scappettone

life is a loose experiment for some, too
empty the earth the hole in its knees,
to transfix lances and persuaded anecdotes, I strew you
world who girds the arms for laurel. Although
too loose the mystery of your lugubrious eyes
although too false the asking on one's knees
I would like with anxiety more live to tell you again: strew
the plants in my soul (a snare), since
I can't move these folded knees anymore. Too much
in sun the life that extinguishes itself, too much in shadow
the ball of wool that led to the cottage, a swollen
sea of your eyelids.

Seeking a response to an unconscious voice
or through her thinking to find it—I saw the muses
bewitch themselves, spreading void veils on their hands
not correcting themselves at the door. Seeking a response
that would reveal, the orgiastic sense of events
the particular darkening of a fate which through
short rips of light one opposes—the one way
the illustrious act: that does not forget, allows
the walls to graze the skin, suffers no estrangement
and does not revolt, against this grinding and
sobbing ill, which is my moon on the face
the smell of angels on my arms, the step certain
and unconcealed: the ruin slow yet accomplished:
a nondetachment from the low things, writing about them
lying down.

What ails my heart who beats so suavely
& hee disconsoles, & ese
solider soundings? you Those
drains I'mprinted there fore I
self-plagued so
ferociously, all have forsaken it! O you're m-y
rampant rabbithearted peri-nerves & a
long hazish canals off my lymph (o life!)
they don't *stop*, thus yes, here I, mai
comyng unto mortae! In all claundors my soul
you propose a cure, I arm you, you,—
find at Suave Word, you, return
to the comprehended saying that makes love stay.

5 Poems for a Poetic

(Reggio Emilia)

I.

Permit me chains of indulgence, save me from the boat that
sinks, calibre of thought oust the argonauts from this
my abode of dimensions unknown; revivify my lips begging
for alms, bring to ash the rest of my days
not so square as to be unable to judge justice, transparent
if you verify it, but by no means a serene exploration.
Where is the who comes, who parts, incomprehensible I remain
and bound and descend through the nocturnal haunts of a farmer: fat
hands short breath crystallemes of noncaring, I don't give a shit!
and fall headlong into your target. Pressing the disgraced shopkeepers
breaking vicissitudes, no—I wanted to say, but it escaped me, the
urine and moon and commerce crystallized innocently
to do away with me—press therefore, sophisticated anguish of the
moons—make me therefore understand! Praxis of the night (a night clever
was the night) praxis of my not finding not understanding not pardoning
the trifle that is my *refrigerator*, battering the beast
that concentrated so steadfastly as to sneeze.
Collision of beasts and landslides, my dreams won't leave
me alone, press therefore the rapport of pleasure,
it's you alone that I seek.

2.

Practically embeasted I stretched out rhinocerous strong on the
hill of your capital: that is: I do not know: I do not want: you are not:
I do not see: I do not stay: not, not, not, not, capital of
my dexterities because I've lost you farmer semantic howler
to the infinite, I don't know if I have been clear, but I don't see you
appear anymore in my arms desolant for the score
that made one wait. What I wanted to say fled
through the window and the softness of your gaze does not corrode
your gift of freshness: thought has nothing to do with it! I don't see
you, I don't have anything to do with it: coalited thought is naught for me but
a coagulation collision of heartblockages up from the parochial head
of secrets. Secret of the night and of the tomb perilous
adversary of those without a moon, your miraculous parochial sculpting
initiates my end and begins another. Clarity desert
of the intellect runner in the vein of *sandwich*, against the
fountain the cherub sits, a crematory of linguistics is the
farce of our credences of our credentials.

3.

Because I sought to be clear. Because I died of you, tireless sleepwalker
my emotions. For the nights that took the prolixities
of a heartblockage I rhymed lush permanent lust. For the
nights impish in the junctures of the nights I truly do not have
end. For the insatiable members for the insensitive beast
for the nights for the look, for the eye that in the breakers
hung itself from the vocabulary, curt recipe for ricotta you watch
and don't see me you hear and despair of me. For the protagonist
who balanced herself weekly I respond to you: I do not have, I do not
see, I do not clarify the weekly responding that I am good.

4.

Because I cannot tell you that I am good. Believe me, there is,
for example, for the critique of things, a sign, in my lips
that you are firm.

Take the pen and learn to watch, risk the cough in the
vestibulary, almost, small circle also, dozens
but what am I saying, hundreds of sterile glances behind my shoulders,
the night instead a rhyming without shoulders.

5.

A sterile night. The light in the oval room permanent. Subdued
screams, your thinking. Crash!, there is light no more. To scream
subdued and gesticulate but not to find any response
is natural is necessary to my rose feet. I have no
ambition to succor itemized sensibilities nor to be I
aired by the latest news: that is: dedicated to truth. What
cruel world this is you cry but don't see that I think seek
that which you can, any juncture, whore with long
sly ears, believe me the battle is naught but a semantic
revolution.

The latest news prevailed in its gaze readily reflected in my queer
body. That is: look: there are three points: the
shoulder broad the neck narrow and the lips are soft.

Versatile smelling together with certain small ambitions I won't say
hidden but evident everyone knows it. Believe me the boats in the
muddled rivers are round: I have nothing more to say,
breath is a strategy for confusing oneself in language, that
if you want, and can, and recollect, and your mind afflicted with
clear meningitis is clear, the assembly prevails in small discussions
sent back to the vocabulary, break my bone pretend that I am like
all of you, who in catatonic language disguise *l'engagement*
of your mother.

What pretty poppies they are. They spiritualize
the grass, which grates cheeses of them.

Rio Claro: mechanized center: flowers (they
have no name) extend a friendly hand, drizzly
and sad (if you are) you extend an arm to the
wind and the rare rain.

Then you sense yourself superceded: they've snatched all
those breasts off the gigantesses! Again you extend
a friendly hand to the umbrella, and frugal
foot to the earth, little monstrous dust
that sneezes. Without an umbrella you cannot
stay: it rains like the damned now that you have taken in
the whole scent of the flowers (if they were there).

You with your whole heart are scared
of air that rouses and loses you;
down for the illiterate facades
disprison the dreams, the blood
in fat drops that you count
falling headlong upon hands
retired from the anguish of knowing
where the air is what it moves why
it speaks, of ills so showered
as to seem, so many things amass
but not one that would disrecord that
dragging of yours for immense days
the night and blood.

There is wind still and all efforts
fail to keep the clearing
steadfast in its design.

I hear the grass tingling, it cannot,
love itself. Save in releasing
scents into air, disobeying
nature.

Boulders brood over snakes which correct
this nascent idyll.

CHRISTOPHER MULROONEY

amphitheater

how you arrive
dodging this and burned by that
or the other way around

pale ocher light
not without indications
and other signs

and here is the story
my story and yours

there once was a man

rondo

Luke the barn
they would say the impressionists

I met a fellow new at a gas station
in the South Bay
Arnold Schoenberg's spitting image

it's just a preserve
not very carefully preserved at all
that was a city

whether you think the barn was a new match
or quite impossibly slow
it went and goes they all go slow
and quick

turnstile

I don't know any about you
that clinches it
one way or another

here she is comin' round the mountain
or gazing up at it

DEVIN JOHNSTON

Crows

Their caw is not
for us, but calls
to corvid, canid,
ringing out
tomorrow's *cras*
and love the dead.

Black lees
against the snow,
a murder crowns
what's left of day.
Riled by shadows
cast in bronze,

they raven trash
and mob the sun,
their wings and bills
compacted as
initials from
the Book of Kells.

Locusts & Wild Honey

Even the dog cocks his ear
when called. Magnetic name:

in a wilderness of sense I clear
a space for pride and shame.

Sunflowers in November

Sunflowers in November
stoop over their own shadows,
stems hooked like bristles
on a card for Cheviot wool.

As pump-jacks nod in the distance,
reservoirs nearly empty,
heavy heads of sunflowers
dream of the rising sun.

Though we may talk of faces,
Helios is the only source
to which this face refers:
a source it can't survive.

LIDIJA DIMKOVSKA

from Macedonian by Ljubica Arsovska & Peggy Reid

Projection

Laurie Anderson had a bad night.
Her bare arms gave the impression of cul-de-sacs in the dark.
The muscles grieved for total darkness.
Darkness, said Laurie, is the projection of the core
which although invisible is the goal of the electronic erection.
Laurie, I believe you met God face to face.
I met him face to face to face. Nobody knew who was addressing whom.
The people were turning to look at the blond in silk stockings,
the blond was turning to look at the nun with her head down.
Everyone thinks that in border situations like this
God looks at the one in black robes. But you, Laurie, know
that he looks at the one looking at the nun
and it's on her silk stockings that he sticks the "God's child" label.
God knows if he also pinches her as well.
But, that's their business. I look at my hands
attacked by love staphylococci.
I'm freezing in my folk-embroidered blouse
because she too was crazy about Indian blouses.
And he was crazy about Levi's
but may darkness swallow me up if I tell him that.
Sweet prohibition, keep Laurie's hands in good shape!
The contents of the bag are emptied into hot water
boiled for thirteen minutes and served with cream.
Then Laurie's aunt tells her Andersen's fairy tales.
Then Laurie's aunt dies
and the old maid is buried in a wedding gown.
Laurie interrupts the priest and sings to her aunt:
In the world beyond a husband is waiting for you,
that's where you'll find your happiness.
You're a bitch, Laurie, and a big one at that!

But I know that you know how your palms itch when you're alone,
when the electricity goes off,
and the silence whirls in your stomach
I know that you know how hard it is
to dress in white after wearing black,
and have your arms not merge into the day
but be signs by the road
and to have nobody, Laurie, nobody travel
down your roads.

Recognition 5

People think that I'm crying.
And I simply wear inappropriate contact lenses
which scratch my eyes in self-observation.
The white of my eye is a map of roads crosscut with rails.
The train that brought you was long ago withdrawn from use.
Have you got sturdy legs for your return to the womb?
Or else a wheelchair?
I have noone to bless my home.
The priests' wives murmur. The dolls are impossible.
All night long they stand on their heads and curse
human values. God pretends to understand them.
But still, I'm not an abstract woman.
Had I been able to enter into you,
your metabolism would have been in order,
and I could have seen the world with eyes undamaged
by inappropriate literature in childhood.
The bells tolled solemnly and the rhythm flowed smoothly.
No, she shouted! My bells toll folk style,
intermingling with the sound of grannyvetka's bell,
Constantine! You're a constant spirit in the little dents along the walls
like these bugs crawling along my conscience.
I became an infanticide. Even the graves die.
His life is empty and the fridge is full.
When the angel flew away an earthquake shook happiness.
Don't cry, don't cry, or we'll call Uncle Freud!
No, it's just my lenses irritating the erotic spot.
And the child is not mine. You know whose it is?
It's … It's … It's … But, you finally fell asleep. Paris is always so close,
I only have to stretch my arm, but he's far away from the Seine.
Wash my eyes with you. Make a path for me, the half-blind woman,
to Notre Dame. Give me the Communion with a finger in my mouth.
Recognize me, damn it, recognize me.

Recognition 6

I was not beaten in a sack.
That's why I can't see you upside down
and still less can I believe in cities
founded in post-war agreements on cultural co-operation.
The fallen hero asks me the time
and the watch, I can see, has grown a small tummy
out of universal awareness I no longer shake hands
but only nod my head. This little body in my sleeve
is proud meat perfect for practical classes in anatomy
in the electronic hospital. I put on your shirt
and I hit my arm against teacher Slobodanka's memoirs.
Every experience is a bit immoral.
You'd better fill the sack with graffiti like this one:
"I'm a happy cube! (-16°c)"
You'd better turn me towards you in your inside pocket
and I'll be repeating it to you, the folk message:
"Take your pocketknife, unstitch the lining
that's where I've hidden the last sin."
But the sack's a good human invention for people like us.
Inside it we're finally three-dimensional,
and time was born just today. Had I known
that birth's brief and breathless
as an international phone call,
I would've been able to learn shorthand
I would've been able to measure the chicken's pulse
as you're filling it with nuclear sky
like a kaleidoscope or a bathtub.
But would I have been able to fill the sack
with gnawed bones without saying to you:
Alesh, you know what? It was on the news
that the assassination attempt against the president
was the deed of noone else but Scheherezade!

Recognition 7

I got up on my left foot and I stood like that
until the floor detached itself from black thoughts.
The foot feels cramp. Thoughts are steps which have migrated
to a cannibal society. Then why do they
say I'm bodiless and a beast on top of that.
I was looking for myself in the glass door—it saw me.
A myopic look corrected by contact lenses,
the only form of body at the end of the century.
The neighbour called me to try on some imported dresses.
I locked myself in her bedroom
and tried on silicon eyes. I didn't know her husband kept them
in mothballs. They smelled of my memory.
If they are too loose, my mother will take them in for you.
And does you mother know how to let out
creatures made to the measure of imported dresses?
And just out of spite I stood on my head all noon
(luckily Balkan women don't suffer from headaches,
the headache, neuro-psychiatrists would say,
is typical of independent women who have remained alone),
out of spite I made you memories, turned you out of home,
reported you to the police. The police caught you,
beat you up, if you're the head of the household—then you're the
            head, he told you,
if not—you need a head. Next time you'd better not leave her on
            her own!
Now we have neither a floor nor a ceiling.
I live in a wall clock and all day long I cuckoo.
When you don't want to know the time
I become nervous and vulgar: I swear and spit.
And it's intolerable, it is, this ease of living,
but what, what do the clinically dead say,
what do they say of, God forgive, existence?

Dental Poem in Golden Lane

On leaving Golden Lane
the men took out their sharp-toothed pocket combs
and briskly smoothed their reflexes
—silver-white like K's visions,
the women tied their sizzling heads in deer-hide scarves
—payments in kind instead of their monthly salary for May,
and I repeated the exercises for a thin neck
clutched in plaster as if in the arms of someone drowning.
In that small house no. 22 the guide stabs his cry at us:
"I'll get myself gold teeth, porcelain alienates me!"
We step with tight lips, the world is a vacuum denture,
the echo of the voice resounds in different languages,
but the ascent wants tongues hanging out, not an installation
of pocket combs, hides and a plaster-wrapped straw.
At night the street is locked
with a golden key, lest K wake as a tourist.
And maybe the mouth full of precious beads
will no longer chatter idly about the gravity underfoot,
but will be as light as a salt-cellar tipped over,
or the anatomical insole of a bride's shoe?
Don't ask me, K. I clean my teeth every night with A's visiting cards,
I plasticise my breath and between my gums
I stratify my own closeness as if in a gutter.
And my neck is made of plaster to prevent my mind from shrivelling,
and my combs are behind my ears so that the rescuer will hear me.
I am not even my own guide through the rooms of the absurd,
that's why neither gold nor porcelain can harm
the enamel of my wisdom tooth. Only these white visiting cards
with black codes in Golden Lane
pick again and again at K's decision:
"Fillings neutralize me, I'll get myself milk teeth."

Mina Assadi was born in northern Iran in 1943. After completing a degree in Media Studies in Tehran, she began working as a journalist and critic for various newspapers and literary journals. She is the author of numerous books of poetry, essays, and short stories, most of which have been published only outside Iran. Her travels to Europe began before the Revolution, but due to censorship, she finally settled in Sweden in 1980. She is still forbidden from entering Iran.

Ilya Bernstein's collection of poetry is called *Attention and Man* (Ugly Duckling Presse, 2003). His poetry, prose, and translations have appeared in *Ars Interpres*, *The Best American Poetry 2005* (forthcoming), *Circumference*, *Fulcrum*, *6x6*, *Persephone*, *Moon City Review*, and *Res*. He is the editor of *Osip Mandelstam: New Translations* (UDP, 2006). He translates for a living and lives in New York City.

David Blair was born in 1970 and grew up in Pittsburgh. He teaches at the New England Institute of Art in Brookline, MA. He has an undergraduate degree in philosophy from Fordham University and an MFA in creative writing from The University of North Carolina, Greensboro. He lives in Medford with his wife Sabrina.

Elena Borta is a freelance literary researcher and translator who has contributed translations from English and Scandinavian languages to various literary and cultural periodicals. She is currently working on a book-length manuscript on fantasy in Mircea Eliade. Borta has been the recipient of a travel grant from the Soros Foundation. Her translations of Ioan Flora with Adam Sorkin have appeared in *Chase Park*, *Visions International*, *Natural Bridge*, *Facets*, *eXchanges*, *Ellipsis*, *Philadelphia Poets*, *Saranac Review*, and *River City*.

Jack Collom teaches ecology-poetics and oversees Project Outreach at the Jack Kerouac School of Disembodied Poetics, where he has been resident faculty for over a decade. His books include *Arguing With Something Plato Said*, *The Task*, and *Entering the City*. He has worked extensively with the Teachers and Writers Collaborative in New York City. He has twice been awarded a National Endowment for the Arts Fellowship. *Red Car Goes By* (a selected poems 1955-2000) was published by Tuumba Press. Collom lives in Boulder, CO.

Phil Cordelli is currently, though tenuously, residing in New York City, New York. He is a member of the Ugly Duckling Presse collective in Red Hook, Brooklyn, where large cruise ships can sometimes be seen. He is also a member of The Pines, which has no real location but www.thepines.blogspot.com. Works of his can be seen in magazines such as *CutBank*, *Pool*, and *Cannibal*; and in books such as *The Pines Volume Three: The Knights of Columbus*.

Sam Cornish lives in Boston and is the author of *1935: A Memoir* (Ploughshares Books) and two books of poems through Zoland Books, *Cross A Parted Sea* and *Folks Like Me*. He is the former Literature Director for the Massachusetts Council on the Arts and Humanities. His book reviews have appeared frequently in *The Christian Science Monitor* and other periodicals.

Joel Craig lives in Chicago, Illinois, working as a graphic designer and deejay. His poems have been published in *Iowa Review*, *Fence*, *Spoon River*, *Bridge* and *MoonLit*, among others. He cofounded and curates The Danny's Reading Series.

Julian Meldon D'Arcy is Professor of English at the University of Iceland. He has written several articles and two books on Scottish literature: *Scottish Skalds and Sagamen* (1996) and *Subversive Scott* (2005). He is currently writing a book on sport literature. He has also translated into English some Icelandic children's books and plays, a book on Icelandic birds, and a collection of stories by one of Iceland's foremost twentieth-century authors, Svava Jakobsdóttir: *The Lodger and Other Stories*.

Lidija Dimkovska was born in 1971 in Skopje, Macedonia. Her prizewinning debut collection *Progenies of the East* was published in 1992, and she has since written three more books of poetry (*Fire of Letters*, *Bitten Nails*, and *Nobel vs. Nobel*) and has edited an anthology of young Macedonian poets. In 2004 she published her prizewinning novel *Hidden Camera*. In 2006 Ugly Duckling Presse published a selection of her poetry *Do Not Awaken Them With Hammers*. She lives and works in Ljubljana, Slovenia.

Valerie Duff earned her masters degree in creative writing from Boston University and Trinity College, Dublin. Her poems have appeared in *Ploughshares*, *Harvard Review*, *Agni*, *Denver Quarterly*, and elsewhere, and her book reviews have appeared in *Salamander*, *Bostonia*, and *PN Review* (UK). She is a regular poetry editor for *Salamander*, and she has received St. Botolph and Massachusetts Cultural Council grants for her poetry. Her short play, *The Means Which Enable Me to Work*, was performed in an Arlington New Plays Festival in 2004. She is a freelance writer and editor and stay-at-home mom living in the Boston area.

Thomas Sayers Ellis cofounded The Dark Room Collective (in Cambridge, Massachusetts); he received his MFA from Brown University in 1995. He is the recipient of a Mrs. Giles Whiting Writers' Award and fellowships from The Bread Loaf Writers' Conference, The Fine Arts Work Center, Yaddo, and The MacDowell Colony. His poems have appeared in *Callaloo*, *The Best American Poetry (1997 and 2001)*, *Grand Street*, *Poetry*, *Tin House*, and numerous anthologies, including *Legitimate Dangers: American Poets of the New Century*. He is the author of *The Maverick Room* (2005), which won the John C. Zacharis First Book Award, *The Good Junk* (*Take Three #1*, 1996), *The Genuine Negro Hero* (2001), and a chaplet, *Song On* (2005). Currently Mr. Ellis is an Assistant Professor of Writing at Sarah Lawrence College and a faculty member of The Lesley University low-residency MFA Program. His *Quotes Community: Notes for Black* Poets is forthcoming from the University of Michigan Press.

Astradur Eysteinsson is professor of Comparative Literature at the University of Iceland (Reykjavik). His publications include co-translations of works by Franz Kafka and Max Frisch into Icelandic, several articles in the general area of literary, cultural, and translation studies, and three books: *The Concept of Modernism* (Cornell UP 1990), *Tvimaeli* (on translation and translation studies, University of Iceland Press 1996) and *Umbrot* (on literature and modernity, University of Iceland Press, 1999). He is also the co-editor (with Daniel Weissbort) of *Translation—Theory and Practice: A Historical Reader* (OUP, 2006).

Ioan Flora—author of fifteen books of poetry, among them *Lecture on the Ostrich-Camel* (1995), *The Swedish Rabbit* (1998), *Medea and Her War Machines* (2000)—died in February 2005 only days after the publication of his final book of poems, the title of which, ironically, was a black-humor play on Manet's *Déjeuner sur l'herbe*—in

Romanian, *Dejun sub iarba* or *Luncheon Under the Grass*. Flora won prizes at the Struga Poetry Festival, from the Writers' Union of the Republic of Moldova, and from both the Romanian Writers' Union and Association of Professional Writers in Romania (ASPRO), among other awards.

Sarah Fox lives in Minneapolis with her husband John Colburn and her daughter Nora. She works as a community outreach facilitator for Parents in Community Action Head Start, as editor of Fuori Editions, as a teacher of poetry and creative writing in schools and literary centers through Minnesota, and as a doula. She's won grants and awards from the National Endowment for the Arts, the Bush Foundation, the Jerome Foundation, and the Minnesota State Arts Board. *Because Why,* her first collection of poems, was published by Coffee House Press.

Benjamin Friedlander's areas of expertise include poetry and poetics, nineteenth- and twentieth-century American literature, and critical theory. He is the author of *Simulcast: Four Experiments in Criticism* (University of Alabama Press, 2004) and coeditor of *Charles Olson's Collected Prose* (UC Press, 1997).

Lyn Hejinian is a poet, essayist, and translator. She was born in the San Francisco Bay Area and lives in Berkeley. Published volumes of her writing include *Writing Is An Aid to Memory, My Life, Oxota: A Short Russian Novel, Leningrad* (written in collaboration with Michael Davidson, Ron Silliman, and Barrett Watten), *The Cold of Poetry*, and *Sight,* written in collaboration with Leslie Scalapino. Some of her most recent books include *A Border Comedy* (Granary Books, 2001), *Slowly* and *The Beginner* (both published by Tuumba Press, 2002), *My Life in the Nineties* (Shark Books, 2003), and *The Fatalist* (Omnidawn, 2003).

Fanny Howe was born in Buffalo, New York, in 1940. She is the author of more than twenty books of poetry and prose. Her recent collections of poetry include *On the Ground* (Graywolf, 2004), *Gone* (2003), *Selected Poems* (2000), *Forged* (1999), *Q* (1998), *One Crossed Out* (1997), *O'Clock* (1995), and *The End* (1992). Howe was the recipient of the 2001 Lenore Marshall Poetry Prize for her Selected Poems. She has also won awards from the National Endowment for the Arts, the National Poetry Foundation, the California Council for the Arts, and the Village Voice, as well as fellowships from the Bunting Institute and the MacArthur Colony. She was shortlisted for the Griffin Poetry Prize in 2001 and 2005.

Daniela Hurezanu has a PhD in romance languages and literatures and taught French for ten years at several universities in the United States. She has published translations in *Metamorphoses, Manoa, Field, Exquisite Corpse, New Orleans Review*, and *Circumference*, and her original work has appeared or is forthcoming in *LittéRéalité, Pacific Review*, and *Prairie Schooner*.

Devin Johnston is the author of two books of poetry, *Aversions* (Omnidawn, 2004) and *Telepathy* (Paper Bark Press, 2001), as well as a number of chapbooks. The latter include a collaboration with the artist Brian Calvin entitled *Looking Out* (Lvng Supplementals, 2004). His book of criticism, *Precipitations: Contemporary American Poetry as Occult Practice*, appeared from Wesleyan University Press in 2002. With Michael O'Leary, he directs Flood Editions, an independent and nonprofit press for poetry.

Henia & Ilona Karmel wrote the poems in this volume as young women of twenty and fifteen in the forced labor camps of World War II. Henia and Ilona were born into an affluent and distinguished family in Krakow. They spoke Polish, Yiddish, and German. They read Hebrew and Western classics as well as Adam Mickiewicz and the contemporary Polish-Jewish poet Julian Tuwim. In a section of Buchenwald set aside for women the sisters sewed the poems into the hems of their dresses. Fanny Howe met Ilona at MIT in the fall of 1978. The poems included here are rough, immediate, emotionally young and determined by early education in rhymed verse.

Esmail Kho'i was born in Mashad, Iran, in 1938. He received his PhD in Philosophy from London University and then left Iran for good in 1983. He is the author of more than twenty volumes of poetry reflecting a variety of styles, as well as several volumes of essays and translations. *Edges of Poetry* and *Outlandia* are selected volumes of his works in English translation. *Voice of Exile*, published in 2002, is his first work of poetry in English.

Tanya Larkin was born in Italy, grew up in Western Pennyslvania, and now lives in Somerville, MA. She was educated at Columbia University and the University of Iowa Writers' Workshop. In 2004 she was a recipient of a Massachusetts Cultural Council Grant. She teaches English at the New England Institute of Art. Her most recent poems have appeared in *The Hat* and *Boog City*. At present, she is working on a novel.

Joan Lindgren translated and edited the work of Argentine poet Juan Gelman for the University of California Press volume *Unthinkable Tenderness* (1997). Having published her translations widely, she is now traveling with the installation art project from Buenos Aires POESIA DIARIA/EVERYDAY POETRY/LA POESIE DE TOUS LES JOURS, a community poetry translation effort (www.poesiadiaria.com).

Rachel Loden's book *Hotel Imperium* (Georgia) was named one of the ten best poetry books of the year by *The San Francisco Chronicle*, which called it "quirky and beguiling." Loden has also published *The Last Campaign*, which won the Hudson Valley Writers' Center Chapbook Prize, and *The Richard Nixon Snow Globe* (Wild Honey Press). Her work has appeared recently in *New American Writing, Jacket, Western Wind: An Introduction to Poetry, Best American Poetry 2005*, and elsewhere. Awards include a Pushcart Prize, a Fellowship in Poetry from the California Arts Council, and a 2006 grant from the Fund for Poetry.

Gian Lombardo is the author of three collections of prose poetry—*Standing Room, Sky Open Again* (Dolphin-Moon Press, 1989 & 1997) and *Of All the Corners to Forget* (Meeting Eyes Bindery, 2004). His translation of the first half of Aloysius Bertrand's *Gaspard de la nuit* was published in 2000, and a translation of Eugène Savitzkaya's *Les règles de solitude* in 2004. He directs Quale Press, which publishes both literary and technology-oriented works. He also teaches courses on book and magazine publishing at Emerson College where he is director of the Publishing Certificate Program.

Work by **John Maloney** has appeared in the *Boston Book Review, The New York Times, North Atlantic Books Anthology, Ploughshares, Poetry, Poetry Northwest*, and *Southern Poetry Review*. His book *Proposal* was published by Zoland Books in 1999.

Poems and translations of **Chris Michalski** have been published or are forthcoming in such journals as *Spoon River Poetry Review*, *Asheville Poetry Review*, *Poetry International*, *RHINO* and *FIRE*. His second film, *weg*, is currently in post-production.

Ange Mlinko's first book *Matinées* was published by Zoland Books in 1999 and was hailed at the time as a Publishers Weekly Book of the Year. Her second collection *Starred Wire* (Coffee House, 2005) was the National Poetry Series award winner. She currently lives outside of New York City with her husband and two young sons.

Born in Argentina in 1942, **Hugo Mujica** left home at nineteen. As a plastic artist in New York during the sixties, he repaired to the same guru as Allen Ginsberg. After meeting Thomas Merton at Gethsemane, Mujica elected the monastic life and spent seven years in silence, discovering the source of his poetry. Now living in Buenos Aires, where he teaches philosophy, he travels Argentina on lecture tours, spending January and February teaching in Madrid. In February, 2006, Mujica became Argentina's second living poet—after Juan Gelman—to have his entire poetic work collected by Seix Barral. The first printing of his *Poesia Completa* sold out within two months.

Christopher Mulrooney has written poems and translations in *The Aroostook Review*, *The Hollins Critic*, *Eclipse* and *Upstairs at Duroc*, criticism in *Parameter*, *Elimae*, and *The Film Journal*, and a volume of verse, *notebook and sheaves* (AmErica House, 2002).

Charles North has published seven collections of poetry, the most recent of which, *The Nearness of the Way You Look Tonight* (Adventures in Poetry), was a finalist for the inaugural Phi Beta Kappa Poetry Award. A new collection, *Cadenza,* is due from Hanging Loose in 2007. He has also published a book of essays on poets, artists and critics, *No Other Way,* and collaborations with the poet Tony Towle and the artist Trevor Winkfield. With James Schuyler he edited the poet/painter anthologies *Broadway* and *Broadway 2*. North is Poet-in-Residence at Pace University in New York City.

Raymond Queneau (1903-1976) was a novelist and poet best known for his works *Exercises in Style*, *Zazie dans le Metro*, and *One Hundred Billion Poems*. He is also renowned for having cofounded in 1960, with François Le Lionnais, OuLiPo (Ouvroir de la Litterature Potentielle), a forum which fostered experimentation based on various types of constraints, the most famous example of which being the total absence of the letter "e" in Georges Perec's novel *La Disparition*.

Born in India in 1965, **Mani Rao** has lived in Hong Kong since 1993. She is the author of six poetry books including *Echolocation* (Chameleon Press, 2003, Hong Kong). Rao's writing can be found in many anthologies and journals including *Wasafiri, Meajin, WestCoastLine, Fulcrum,* and *Iowa Review.* In Hong Kong, Rao co-founded a poetry reading series and hosted a weekly poetry program on the radio. She was the Writer-in-residence for the University of Iowa International Programs and visiting fellow at the UI International Writing Program, 2005. Her multi-media work is on www.manirao.com

Barbara Jane Reyes was born in Manila, Philippines, and raised in the San Francisco Bay Area. She received her undergraduate education at UC Berkeley, and her MFA at San Francisco State University. She is the author of *Gravities of Center* (Arkipelago, 2003) and *Poeta en San Francisco* (Tinfish, 2005), for which she received the James Laughlin Award of the Academy of American Poets. Her work appears or is forthcoming in *Action Yes, Asian Pacific American Journal, Chain, Crate, How2, Interlope, New American Writing, North American Review, Parthenon West Review, Shampoo Poetry, Tinfish,* and *Versal,* among others. She lives and works in Oakland, CA.

Amelia Rosselli—poet, journalist, musician, musicologist, and composer—was born in Paris in 1930. Her family was forced to move between France, England, and the United States after the 1936 assassination of her father by Fascist order; she eventually settled in Rome in 1950. She is the author of 8 volumes of poetry in Italian, including *Bellicose Variations* (*Variazioni belliche, 1959–1961*) and *Hospital Series* (*Serie ospedaliera, 1963–1965*), from which the poems in this annual were drawn, as well as of *Sleep: Poems in English (1953–1966),* and various polylingual works gathered in *Primi scritti 1952–1963* (*Early Writings, Guanda 1980*). She died in 1996.

Jennifer Scappettone's current book projects include *From Dame Quickly* (poems), *Locomotrix: Selected Poetry of Amelia Rosselli* (translations), *Venice and the Digressive Invention of the Modern* (a critical study of the obsolescent metropolis as a crucible for modernism), and *Exit 43* (an archaeology of the landfill and opera of pop-ups in progress, commissioned by Atelos Press). She is an Assistant Professor of English at the University of Chicago.

Born in 1973 in Karlsruhe, **Silke Scheuermann** has received numerous awards and critical acclaim for her poetry and short fiction. Her third book of poems and her first novel are both due to be released some time next year.

Born in Ankara in 1961, **Zafer Şenocak** has been living since 1970 in Germany, where he has become a leading voice in the German discussions on multiculturalism and national and cultural identity, and a mediator between Turkish and German culture. A widely published poet, essayist, journalist, and editor, he has won several prestigious literary awards in Germany. His works have been translated into Turkish, English, French, Dutch, and Hebrew.

Patricia Smith is the author of four books of poetry: *Teahouse of the Almighty*, the 2005 National Poetry Series award winner, *Close to Death*; *Big Towns, Big Talk*—both published by Zoland Books—and *Life According to Motown*. Her work has been widely anthologized and performed worldwide. Author of the critically acclaimed history *Africans in America* and the award-winning children's book *Janna and the Kings*, Smith is currently working on *Fixed on a Furious Star*, a biography of Harriet Tubman. A Cave Canem faculty member and former McEver Chair in Writing at Georgia Tech University, Smith is also a four-time National Poetry Slam champion.

Adam J. Sorkin's recent books of translation include Daniela Crasnaru's short stories translated with the author, *The Grand Prize and Other Stories* (Northwestern UP, 2005), and Marin Sorescu's, *The Bridge*, translated with Lidia Vianu (Bloodaxe Books)—the winner of the 2005 Corneliu M. Popescu Prize for European Poetry Translation of The Poetry Society, London. Sorkin's version of Magda Cârneci, *Chaosmos*, is now out from White Pine Press, and Mariana Marin, *Paper Children* (with various collaborators), from Ugly Duckling. He received a 2005-2006 NEA Poetry Fellowship.

Niloufar Talebi was born in London to Iranian parents, and schooled in Iran, Europe, and the United States. She received a BA in Comparative Literature from UC Irvine, and an MFA in Writing and Literature from Bennington College. She has worked in theater and film since 1991. She founded The Translation Project in 2003 to bring contemporary Iranian literature to the world stage in multiple languages and media. Her translations have been anthologized and published in *Two Lines, Poetry International, Agni on-line, Circumference,* and *Hogtown Creek Review*, and she was the guest editor of the Spring 2006 issue of *Rattapallax. An Anthology of Contemporary Iranian Poetry Around the World,* which she edited and translated, is forthcoming in 2008.

Jónas Þorbjarnarson was born 1960 in Akureyri in northern Iceland, and grew up there. He has studied classical guitar, physical therapy, philosophy, art history and French, but lives and works as a poet. He now divides his time mainly between Reykjavik, Iceland, and Italy. He has brought out seven books of poetry. A number of his poems have appeared in translation in several languages.

Meg Tyler has published poems in such journals as *Agni, Kenyon Review,* and *Harvard Review*.

Jacqueline Waters is the author of a book, *A Minute without Danger* (Adventures in Poetry, 2001), and a chapbook, *The Garden of Eden a College* (A Rest Press, 2004). Her work has appeared in *Chicago Review, The Poker, 6x6,* and other magazines. She was born in Jersey City, New Jersey, and currently lives in Greenpoint, Brooklyn.

Elizabeth Oehlkers Wright's translations of contemporary German poets has been featured in *The Seneca Review, Delos, Agni,* and *Another Chicago Magazine* among others. Winner of Agni's William J. Arrowsmith Translation Award, she has received fellowships from the NEA, the American Literary Translators Association, and the University of Arkansas Fulbright College. A selection of her translations of Şenocak will appear in the *PIP Anthology of World Literature of the 20th Century,* forthcoming from Green Integer Books.

Dean Young has published seven books of poems, most recently *Elegy on Toy Piano* which was a finalist for the 2006 Pulitzer Prize. A new book *embryoyo* will be published by Believer Books in the next year. He is a permanent faculty member at the Iowa Writers' Workshop although good luck finding his office.

Photograph by Nat Pease

As editor and publisher of Zoland Books for fifteen years, Roland Pease published such writers as Ha Jin, Kevin Young, Anne Porter, William Corbett, Lisa Jarnot, and John Yau. He currently serves as fiction and poetry editor of Steerforth Press and its Zoland Books imprint.